D0587712

And you hath He quickened, who were dead in trespasses and sins; wherein in times past ye walked according to the course of this world, according to the prince of the power of the air, the spirit that now worketh in the children of disobedience: among whom also we all had our conversation in times past in the lusts of our flesh, fulfilling the desires of the flesh and of the mind; and were by nature the children of wrath, even as others.

But God, who is rich in mercy, for His great love wherewith He loved us, even when we were dead in sins, hath quickened us together with Christ, (by grace ye are saved;) and hath raised us up together, and made us sit together in heavenly places in Christ Jesus: that in the ages to come He might show the exceeding riches of His grace in His kindness toward us through Christ Jesus.

For by grace are ye saved through faith; and that not of yourselves: it is the gift of God: not of works, lest any man should boast.

Ephesians 2:1–9

Reaping with Joy

Isabel Chapman

Marshall Pickering

Marshall Morgan and Scott
Marshall Pickering
3 Beggarwood Lane, Basingstoke, Hants RG23 7LP, UK

Copyright © 1987 Isabel Chapman
First published in 1987 by Marshall Morgan and Scott Publications Ltd
Part of the Marshall Pickering Holdings Group
A subsidiary of the Zondervan Corporation

British Library CIP Data

Chapman, Isabel
  Reaping with joy.
  1. Evangelistic work
  I. Title
  269′.2′0924   BV3790

  ISBN 0-551-01514-4

Text set in Plantin by Brian Robinson, Buckingham
Printed in Great Britain by Richard Clay Ltd, Bungay, Suffolk

Acknowledgements

I wish to express my sincere thanks to Dick Purcell, who gave himself unstintingly to the hard labour of converting my diary-type manuscript into book form. Without his help, knowledge and patient endurance, I would have been unable to present this book. To Mary, Dick's wife, who patiently stood by him in prayers and intercession, bless you and thank you Mary. To Sally, his daughter, who helped with the word processing, and to Mrs Heather Harris whose quiet efficiency converted masses of manuscript into orderly typescript, my grateful thanks.

Ron and Jean Taylor, who have stood faithfully, as firm as rocks behind me over the years, have been a great source of strength and encouragement. Without their help in the ministry correspondence, I would have been unable to fulfil the itinerant ministry to which the Lord has called me. Please accept my deep gratitude and thanks.

For Daphne, my helper and companion, I thank God daily. Thank you for being just you and allowing me to be just me.

Sincere and grateful thanks to my mother and all who faithfully stood by me in prayer. The fervent prayer of the righteous availeth much. Hallelujah!

God is my provider, but He provides through His Body. I wish to express my deep gratitude to those who have stood by this ministry and helped financially with love gifts and through the purchase of books and tapes. None of our labours will go unrewarded by the God of Israel.

Chapter One

I was home! The familiar Norwich streets flashed past the windows of the taxi but we didn't stop at the bungalow in The Paddocks. It was no longer mine and in that sense I had no home any more. In fact, I hadn't got much in the way of the world's goods. When my heavenly Father told me to go to the Philippines ten months earlier, He also told me to sell my house, car and all my possessions except for the contents of a suitcase. In the Philippines, I saw so many needs, that I shared all the money I had with my Filipino brethren. A large part of the value of the bungalow had gone to provide a big twelve-seater jeepney, essential transport for the Orphanage and Bible school at San Fernando. Nevertheless, I had come back much richer than when I left. My experiences had given me an unshakeable conviction that God was truly my Father and would meet all my needs from His inexhaustible store.

The tremendous adventures in the Philippines, which had taken me from modern cities to primitive villages, where no white woman had ever been, had been accompanied everywhere by the awesome evidence of God's supernatural power at work. I had gone with no pre-arranged plan, with no contacts in the country, nothing but an address taken from a record sleeve and a picture of one of the group who had made the record. But God had a plan, which required only obedience to bring it into operation; and so from Manila to San Fernando to Tabuk and the mountains of Kalingo Apayao, to Dagupan and the offshore islands, I was aware of God's leading at every stage. He took me, a three-months-old Christian, who knew little of the Bible, had never preached a sermon and with no understanding of the culture, languages or thought forms of the people and He worked through me.

Never to be forgotten events, fixed like milestones on the road I had travelled in the past year, assured me that His programme incorporated events which I could not have known about and that His power would be manifested to meet the need in seemingly impossible situations. Like the fact that the very first week I was there coincided with a crusade which provided the basic Bible teaching that lifted my appreciation of the power of God's word and the authority delegated to every believer to use the name of Jesus. This happy coincidence provided help in an area where God knew I needed to be built up. Or the time when I first met the primitive mountain people; I did not feel that I could ever relate to them, let alone love them. But His Spirit fell on me and filled me with a deep love for them. On another occasion, I had to speak to an unruly crowd of prisoners in San Fernando jail. I was quite unable to get their attention or to think what to say, but God who had brought me there, spoke through me and all one hundred and thirty men were quietened, brought to repentance and received an individual experience of God. Afterwards, I had very little idea of what I had said.

Not only had I not preached before going to the Philippines, I had never prayed for anyone asking God to heal them, but in a village plagued by endemic goitre God led me to place my hand on a woman's swollen neck and the lump began to dissolve under my hand. I was incredulous! As I doubted the lump grew back. A feeling of remorse that my doubt should rob this woman and thwart God's work swept over me and I cried out to God to forgive me for not believing. The lump disappeared. There had been other milestones and doubtless there would be many more as I made myself unreservedly available. I knew God wasn't finished with me yet.

Back in England, I knew that my future lay in the mind of God. My Lord, who had taken care of me yesterday and today, would lead me and take care of me tomorrow and every day, until He returned to take me to be with Him for ever. I had already learned that He did not usually reveal the details of His long-range plan for my future, but that what I had to do was to walk each day with Jesus and the design would slowly unfold. I knew from the Bible how astonishingly long-term His plans for me were; they stretched from 'before the foundations of the world', to 'the gathering together of all things in Christ' (Eph. 4:4–10). All I wanted was to walk in the perfect will of my Father and fulfil what He was calling me to do.

'This is it.' The taxi driver interrupted my thoughts. We had stopped. I paid him, took my much-travelled suitcase and rang the doorbell. In a moment I was embracing Maria who had warmly invited me to stay while I waited on the Lord for directions. We had been new Christians together in Zion church twelve months before, sharing the strangeness as well as the joy of exploring this new dimension of living into which we had been reborn. Now there were new experiences to be shared and after she had brought me up to date on happenings in Norwich, I began the process, which was to become very familiar, of trying to find words to crystallise the whirl of activities through which the Lord had taken me since we had last met. We talked and talked until the weariness of travel finally won and sleep could no longer be denied.

9

Chapter Two

Norwich was the city from which I had gone to the Philippines and the place to which I had returned, because it was where all those friends lived who had been associated with my coming to know Jesus, who had prayed with me and encouraged me and with whom I was worshipping when God called me to go. As I renewed old friendships, I met again one family, who had been clients of mine when I had been an insurance agent. They became a great encouragement to me in the period of waiting to see where the Lord was going to direct me next. Ron, who was an immigration officer at the airport, lived with his wife Jean at Mulbarton, six miles from the city. Through his kindness, God used him to meet a need I had not recognised. One aspect of having a home is that you have an address; I had no home, so it was going to be very difficult for people to contact me. Ron not only offered the use of his address but also help in dealing with the correspondence which, though I did not realise it then was going to grow beyond what I could have coped with on my own.

It was good that the Lord was taking care of such practical things, because my mind was filled with the experiences I had had in the Philippines and I wanted to share them with my own countrymen. I wanted everyone to know that Jesus is the name above all names. I wanted everyone to know that the Bible really is true. I wanted everyone to know that Jesus is coming back soon. I wanted everyone to know that Jesus heals today. I could not keep my mouth shut. I was bursting with enthusiasm. But I was an unknown woman with few Christian connections in Norwich and none in the country at large. No opportunities to speak to groups were forthcoming where I was: I wondered what surprise God had in store. It came in the shape of an invitation to a wedding.

A wedding in Zion Church was always a joyful occasion though to this bride's aunt and uncle, the freedom of the worship and the simplicity of the service were totally new and unexpected. When I was introduced to Geoffrey and Tina at the reception and asked what I had been doing in the Philippines, they were even more astonished. They were keen to hear more and invited me to their home in Devon.

Geoffrey Campbell-Black is an artist, well known for his drawings and paintings of wild life. Their home was hidden deep in rural Devon, approached along narrow lanes set between high banks. It was a beautiful place, chosen for its peaceful studio and its access to the artist's favourite subjects. On the surface, it seemed that God had taken me from somewhere I was known and accessible to a few people, to where I was out of contact with the whole world: but I was soon to discovere that there were two reasons why I was there. The first was that the Holy Spirit had been working in the hearts of many people who were longing to know God in a deeper and more personal way. Tina was a member of a housegroup which met regularly for prayer and Bible study. They asked me to speak at their next meeting and this invitation led to many more as news spread of the great things God was doing.

Jesus had commanded the disciples of the early church,

Go ye into all the world and preach the gospel to every creature. He that believeth and is baptised shall be saved: but he that believeth not shall be damned. And these signs shall follow them that believe; in my name shall they cast out devils; they shall speak with new tongues; they shall take up serpents; and if they drink any deadly thing, it shall not hurt them; they shall lay hands on the sick and they shall recover.

(Mark 16:15–18)

As they walked in obedience to the words which Jesus had spoken, we read in the Acts of the Apostles how God confirmed His word with signs following. I determined to walk in obedience to the words of my Saviour, in the same way as the early disciples had done. As I did so the Lord was confirming His word with signs following for me, in the same way as He had done with the early church.

At all the meetings, I told about what I had seen and experienced in the Philippines, my personal testimony to God's love and power. It made no difference whether it was in someone's home, in a church or in a restaurant, the name of Jesus was as powerful to save and heal as I had seen it to be on the other side of the world.

The Devon people opened their heart to me. I was welcomed with love and practical kindness all over the South Hams. People would set up meetings for me in their own homes and invite their neighbours. It never concerned me whether there were many or few, nor did it seem to matter to the Holy Spirit whose presence was always evident.

It was a time of revival in the district. Hundreds of people turned from the evil ways of the world and became born again of the Spirit of God, most were also baptised in the Holy Spirit with the evidence of speaking in other tongues and many were set free from the devil's bondage of sickness, so many, that I cannot now remember all the details. Some, however, were special and lodged in my memory, and some wrote to me telling me how they had been healed and describing, from their viewpoint, what it was like to encounter God in such a real way.

I thought of Florence and the way I had met her and become part of God's plan for her family. She reminded me about this, after we had known each other for some time. 'You remember, Isabel, when you first came to the village it was to pray for one of our neighbours who was very ill and I was in the room when you arrived? Well, I was there to check whether you were a faith healer and the others, who were present, were watching my face to see how I reacted when you prayed.' I thought back to the occasion; I had been quite unaware that I was being appraised. Florence, of course, quickly found that I was no psychic but that my ministry was centred on the Lord Jesus Christ. She wanted to hear more. 'Can you come round and speak at our farm? We have a lovely big room, which we've made by knocking down a dividing wall, and the redecoration has just been finished. It would be a wonderful way of dedicating the room, because we believe the Lord wants us to use it in this way.' I gladly accepted but neither of us knew what a blessing that was going to be for the family.

At the first meeting, forty or so people gathered and among those with whom I prayed afterwards was Beryl, who worked for Florence in the house. To her great joy, the Lord healed the hiatus hernia from which she had been suffering. This was not, however, the first healing that had been experienced by that household. Soon after their marriage, Herbert and Florence had moved from Herbert's family farm and set up house a few miles away in Stokenham Barton. Herbert knew that the Lord had led him to choose this place and he and Florence settled down to making a success of the mixed arable and stock farm and bringing up their family of four children, which from time to time was ·increased by the addition of foster children in need of a loving home and by drug addicts trying to get free of their addiction.

After seven good years, Herbert began to feel very unwell. Every month, he would suffer from what seemed like a bad attack of flu. High fever would be accompanied by aching joints and a general weariness which made continuing to work impossible for days at a time. His doctor diagnosed brucellosis, a common disease of cattle which can be transmitted to man. He did not hold out much hope of a cure. But a friend had told them that Jesus was still healing people today and showed them the Scriptures. They believed the word of God and took their stand on it and Jesus healed him. All physical symptoms had gone and with them the dreadful depression which had so blighted both their lives.

All this had happened two years before I had arrived in Devon and now, on my next visit to the farmhouse for a second meeting. I found that Beryl had been so happy and grateful that God had healed her that she wanted everyone else to have the same experience. 'Wouldn't it be good', she said to Florence, 'if Mr Rew asked Isabel to pray for his back'. Florence agreed that it certainly would be good and passed the message on. Here is Herbert's own story as he recounted it to me in a letter.

In December 1981, you came to our area and subsequently came to our house, where on a few occasions a number of people came to hear your testimony and to receive healing as you prayed for them in the name of the Lord Jesus Christ. As a young man I had abused my back, as one orthopaedic doctor told me I had worn out the vertebrae in my back. Consequently I was very restricted in my movements and if I was not careful then I suffered back pain for a period. I have twice spent periods encased in a plaster jacket, and have had to wear a steel brace to restrict my movements and prevent further damage.

Following one of the meetings in our home in February I told you about my back explaining, that I had not asked the Lord to renew my back because I felt so thankful to him for healing me of the brucellosis. In a way, I felt that I had received more than my share of His blessings. But you prayed with me and I was aware of things happening in my back and I am confident that my back was renewed. I put the brace away from that evening. Since that time I can do things that I have been unable to do for twenty years. One example is particularly worthy of note. Just three days after the renewal of my back, I was erecting some sheep fencing and I could see that an old iron hay rack would be ideal to stop one hole in the fence. The hay rack was heavy, certainly much too heavy for some one with a suspect back. I picked it up and placed it where it was required. No problem!

If we receive miracles in our life then we should be aware that the devil will wish to challenge us. This happened to me in a very dramatic way at the beginning of August. I was at a cattle market intending to buy some cattle when my back started to feel uncomfortable. As time went on, I had real pain in my back such as I had not experienced since my healing. I moved around but the pain persisted. I finished the business I intended to do and got into my Land Rover and drove for about a mile with the pain getting worse and worse to the point at which it was almost unbearable. I must confess that for a moment I began to doubt. Then I reasoned that if my back is renewed it could not have gone wrong. Then I realised that it was the devil attacking me. There and then I said, 'I command you evil spirit in the name of Jesus to depart from me and leave me alone'. The pain stopped immediately and I have not felt it since. I could show anyone the exact spot on the road where it happened.

Praise the Lord for His power over the devil and that it was revealed to me who my enemy was.

I was greatly encouraged by this letter. I understood how much it meant to Herbert that he would no longer be in pain every time he drove the tractor and that he would no longer have a feelings of uselessness through having to stand back from a simple job that required lifting and ask someone else to do it. But more than that, I knew that the whole family would not, in future, be dependent on an Isabel Chapman to come and pray with them; they now had an assurance that God was willing to heal them and they knew how to ask.

When this next letter came, short and to the point, it recalled an elderly lady, who asked me to visit her in Torquay, because she was too ill to come to a meeting. She was facing a bleak future, imprisoned in a wheelchair and completely dependent on other people. Melvina wrote on 27 August 1982:

On 1st April this year I had a stroke and was paralysed down my right side. I could not move. I was told by the doctor and nurses that I would never be able to walk or cope with stairs again and that I would be confined to a wheelchair for the rest of my life.

You called on me and prayed and thanks be to God, three days after your visit I started to walk and I have now fully recovered. I am remembering you in my prayers.

Like Herbert, Richard had been born again of the Spirit of God many years before we met but he had been taught that miracles ceased when the Apostles died. He had been suffering from a painful stomach condition, which had been daignosed as an ulcer about eighteen months before he came to the meeting where I was speaking. In spite of treatment with a variety of drugs the condition was no better and just before I met him, his treatment had to be suspended because he had developed an allergic reaction to his medication. His doctor was waiting for the drug rash to subside before starting on a new course of treatment. He wrote, from his home in Salcombe Water:

While the rash was still going down, and everything I ate seemed like red hot gravel going into my stomach (which according to my wife makes a man very bad tempered) I heard about a meeting to be held in Kingsbridge with a young lady called Isabel Chapman. I was already a born again Christian, but had never come across present day healing, having been taught that healing, speaking in tongues etc., all finished with the Apostles' ministry. Looking through the Bible again, I could find no foundation for this teaching and I determined to go along and decide for myself.

I found your testimony very stirring, and the way you gave all the credit to Jesus and the genuine love you had for people, convinced me that this was certainly of the Lord. So, with many others that night, I went forward to be prayed for. You asked me what I required from the Lord, and as I had been feeling my lack of power as a lay preacher, I asked that I might have the power of the Holy Spirit in my preaching and that the ulcer might be healed.

You asked if I spoke in tongues and I replied that I did not. You asked if I wanted to and my answer was, 'Not particularly'. I thought that speaking in tongues was a gift I could well do without. At this point you asked the Lord to heal me, prayed in a language I could not understand, then thanked the Lord for healing me. Your parting words were, 'Exercise your faith, brother!'

Off I went to exercise my faith, which I did for a week and nothing happened. The pain was still as bad as ever.

The rash had now gone, so I went back to the doctor and asked for the new course of treatment. He said it would be ready in a few days. Before I collected this, there was a house meeting at Malborough, about three miles from us. By this time I had analysed my thoughts and had repented before God that I should have dictated to Him what sort of gift I should have or not have. (Remember I had not really wanted the speaking in tongues.) I just prayed to God asking Him to forgive this sin. I also said, 'I'm going to Malborough on 31st March and I'm going to ask Isabel to pray for me again. I'm going to tell all the people there what I am asking you to do, and I expect you to heal me in the power of Jesus' name.'

You prayed very lovingly as before. I didn't feel any different and there was no feeling of anything happening to my body. But there were no doubts and I knew that He would heal me. And sure enough, breakfast next morning went down perfectly; there was no pain. Praise the Lord. As I write this it is now September 1982, and I have had six months of a new awareness of God's power and love. Our God, The Father, the Son, the Holy Spirit, are the same today as in the days of the Apostles.

Chapter Three

In the Philippines, I had worked with missionaries and with members of the indigenous Protestant church, and I found, that what I received from the Holy Spirit and what I understood from the Bible, seemed completely acceptable. Indeed it never occurred to me that anyone would complain about what was so basic and what came so directly from the Scripture. In the South Hams, I accepted invitations from every group who asked me to speak; most were composed of people from different denominational backgrounds but sometimes they were predominantly members of a particular group or church. However, I made no distinction, I spoke a similar message to them all, and always with the same result; Jesus confirmed His word with signs following and in most places this gracious work of God was accepted without debate.

Just a year after I had arrived in Devon, I shared my testimony at a house fellowship in the usual way and, when I had finished speaking, invited those present to respond to what they had heard. Again the expected happened and some were saved, some filled with the Holy Spirit and some were healed. I was, therefore, surprised to receive a message from the minister of the church to say that he was not at all happy about what he had heard had taken place and wanted to see me at his home.

As I walked down the street, counting off the house numbers, looking for the minister's front door, I felt very nervous about the prospect of this interview. I racked my brains to think of anything I might have said that evening which was any different from what I had said many times before. I was received politely, told to be seated, and listened while the minister launched into his objections to what I had said. I had been wrong to base any teaching on Mark 16:15–18. Obviously sensing a theological lightweight, he told me, with patient emphasis, that these verses were not in the original writings and should not have been printed in the Bible. Tongues, he believed, were only for the early church and today's tongues were of the devil and he would never allow them to be spoken in his church. He had a lot to say about healing, of which the substance was, that God chose to heal only on very special occasions: it was not His will to heal everybody: what I was doing was very wrong. I had been misguided and would cause a lot of people great hurt by giving them a false hope of healing, when sickness was part of God's plan to draw people to Him. I could only say, in reply, that my only motive was to do what was right in the sight of God. He had been to university and studied theology. He was a man of God in charge of a large church. I did not have the words with which to argue or any sense that it would be right for me to do so. In any case, his manner did not really invite a reply, so that when he finished speaking, I stood up, shook hands, and said 'Goodbye' in as firm a voice as I could manage.

I felt devastated. I hurried home, my mind reeling with all sorts of fears and doubts. If it were not God's will to heal everyone, and I prayed and asked Him to heal them, then I might be praying against God's will for that person and if that were so, how would I know when to pray and when not to pray? But more seriously still, if the last part of St Mark's Gospel should not have been in the Bible, how would I know if there were other mistakes that I did not know about. The questioning went round and round in my head. I had thought I was standing on a rock but now it appeared to be shifting sand. It had not felt like shifting sand but perhaps I was too inexperienced to judge.

I knew there was only one place where I could find answers to my confusion; I closed the door of my room and got down on my knees before my Father in heaven. I began to pray, and as I always did, when seeking direction about what to ask, I started to pray in tongues. But even that was denied me as I remembered how strongly the minister had spoken against it. I was hurt and confused not knowing what to do or say, so I just cried. As I lay on the floor weeping before the Lord, the Holy Spirit took over and it was as if He were crying out in tongues on my behalf. The Scripture reference Proverbs 30:5 was implanted in my mind: it was not a verse I knew. I opened my Bible and read:

Every word of God is pure, He is a shield unto them that put their trust in Him

This was the answer. This is what God says about His word. As my tears ceased flowing, I began to think about the Acts of the Apostles. They spoke in other tongues, they cast out devils in the name of Jesus and they laid their hands on the sick and they were healed. To complete the list, there was the incident when Paul was bitten by a poisonous snake and was unharmed. I could now see that these acts were made manifest because of the Apostles' obedience to the words of Jesus recorded by Mark. I continued to pray in tongues for a long time until suddenly all the hurt and confusion lifted from me. Through the following week, the Lord kept bringing portions of Scripture to my attention, showing me that I could trust every word in the Scriptures. In one of Paul's Epistles I read:

All scripture is given by inspiration of God, and is profitable for doctrine, for reproof, for correction, for instruction in righteousness; that the man of God may be perfect, thoroughly furnished unto all good works.

(2 Tim. 3:16)

This painful incident made me realise how much my day to day fellowship with the Lord depended on reading the Bible and really knowing, beyond the shadow of a doubt, that it was God's word. He had strengthened my confidence in it and I now knew, that in whatever it plainly stated, I must do what it said. I resolved not to be swayed by merely human ideas, however educated the man or woman was who held them. There were still a lot of questions which remained unanswered; I did not know why some I prayed with to receive the baptism in the Holy Spirit did not speak in tongues, or why some who were sick were not healed. But I knew that the Lord would answer all these questions and give me greater understanding as time went on, because He has promised in His word that 'those who hunger and thirst after righteousness shall be filled'.

Invitations to speak arrived almost every day, and as I continued in the way that the Lord taught me, many were stepping out of the Kingdom of Darkness, He was baptising many in the Holy Spirit and healing and delivering many who were bound by the devil. Jesus was daily doing those things, which He had promised in the last chapter of St Mark's Gospel.

In the revival which had taken place, many people had made a commitment to Jesus: they had repented and confessed that Jesus is Lord. Some were members of churches or house fellowships and some had no previous affiliation. For some weeks, the Lord had been reminding me that there was a requirement in His word, which I had not yet covered: Jesus had said:

He that believeth and is baptised will be saved

(Mark 16:16)

In the Philippines, before we left a village where we had been evangelising, the Lord always led us to baptise the new converts. We would find a natural pool, usually the place where they went daily to bathe, and the Filipino pastor who travelled with me, or the local pastor, would wade into the water and immerse each of the new Christians.

I felt that the Lord was saying, quite strongly, that the new converts in Devon should have the same opportunity. I telephoned those few whose names I knew, pointing out what Scripture said about the need for baptism and asked them to pray about what they should do about it. I remembered that a church in which I had spoken had a baptismal pool, and this seemed more suited to the English climate than an outdoor venue. I telephoned the minister to ask for the use of it, but to my surprise received a blunt refusal. How, I wondered could any Bible-believing Christian not want to see the completion of the work of regeneration in these new Christians? Then some of those whom I had asked to pray about it had consulted their ministers and were told that, if they had been baptised as infants, it would be unnecessary and wrong to be baptised again.

In my simplicity, I was walking into an ecclesiastical minefield. I had believed that everything in churches was done in accordance with Scripture, whatever the denomination. Again, I was accused of leading people astray. I was surprised and saddened when a vicar, whom I respected and loved and with whom, on other matters, I found complete agreement, was adamant on this point. He said that it was the practice of the church to baptise infants and it was a very ancient tradition. 'But', I said, 'a baby can't repent, and the Bible, the Word of God says nothing about baptising babies. Surely, the time to baptise is after, not before, repentance.' He became angry at my refusal to accept what I saw as man-made rules. I found I had to be direct about this, so I said, 'Jesus has called me to walk in obedience to His word and I must not bow the knee to any man-made religious ideas'. That, sadly, ended the conversation. I did not recognise that I had any room for a more flexible attitude; not only was the Bible clear, I also had a continual prompting from the Holy Spirit to act on it. Any compromise at this point, would, I knew diminish my usefulness to God and to people.

I had taken a straightforward view of what the Bible said about baptism, but it was now clear that one denomination at least did not see it that way. It was not very long before the word had been spread and other denominations were showing that, on this issue, they were united against me. After this, I was conscious that barriers were being raised against me: nothing I said or did seemed to be right any more. The devil took the opportunity to whisper negative thoughts into my mind, 'This is the end of your ministry'. 'Go back to your insurance job'. 'You could go to church on Sundays and be a quiet little Christian'. As if in response, I found flooding into my mind prophetic words that had been spoken over me ten months after I had become a Christian. In a large church in America, a stranger walked over to me and began to prophesy over me words that I did not fully understand at the time. The service had been recorded and I was given a transcript afterwards, which I had kept in the hope that one day I would see the relevance of it. When I looked it out, I found that the part which had just come to mind, was in the middle of the prophecy. The words were:

I have picked you and lifted you up because of your obedience and because of your heart. I have set you in a realm of victory. My word shall find a stable place in your heart wherever you go. You may feel as Jeremiah when he said, 'Lord, I am only a youth; they will not listen to me'. But I tell you, that Israel had hardened her heart at that time and would not listen to the truth of her deliverance. As for you, I shall take you and I shall confound the men who set themselves as the Scribes and Pharisees and Sadducees of this day. I shall show the revelation of Jesus Christ in you, and you shall be used in this day. For there are those whose hearts have been hardened by the education they have received, because of the ways of the world that have been taught them, and they have closed their hearts to the truth. But I shall take delight in you, my daughter, because of the simplicity of my word in your heart, because of the truth that is within you.

The Scribes, Sadducees and Pharisees were the religious leaders of Jesus' day. They followed with rigour and sincerity a system which was supposed to be based on Scripture but really included much traditional teaching that had been added over the centuries. Some like Nicodemus acknowledged Jesus, but most were hostile to Him. Jesus had harder things to say about them, than about any other group, because of their leadership role (Matt. 23:12, Luke 11:52) and self-righteousness (Luke 18:11). The Lord had foreseen that I would meet their present day equivalents, who still reject the words of Jesus, and 'by their tradition make the commandment of God of none effect'. The scripture says 'Repent and be baptised' (Acts 2:38); a baby cannot repent, and without repentance, no amount of water can wash away sin. Each individual must come to the place of repentance, turn from the evil ways of the devil and the world, and make a conscious decision to follow Jesus and live his life in accordance with His word. This can only be done when one has matured enough to understand. By faith, we invite the Holy Spirit to come and dwell within us. He puts the desire in our hearts to read the Bible by which our minds get washed and cleansed and renewed by

the washing of the water of the word

(Eph. 6:26)

Those who administer baptism to babies may have very good intentions, and may try to impose safeguards, but there is no blessing when the word of God is disobeyed. This disobedience brings with it a 'strong delusion' (1 Thess. 2:11) by which people are deceived into believing that they are safe for eternity because they had been baptised as babies. So, the actions of today's Pharisees lead to millions of people failing to face up to the most important decision they need to make in the whole of their life.

One of the house fellowships which some of the new converts had joined wished to go ahead with a baptism and were happy that any new Christians should participate. We fixed an afternoon and prayed for fine weather. When we arrived on Paignton beach, the morning rain had rolled away, and we were greeted by the biggest and brightest rainbow I had ever seen. It spanned the bay in a gigantic arc, its colours as brilliant and clearly defined as a child's drawing. 'God's bow in the clouds' is a sign of the covenant-making God, who keeps His word. It was as though He was smiling down on His children of the new covenant as they obeyed His word. The sea was to be our baptismal pool, we now had a chancel arch higher than the greatest cathedral but we had no pulpit! So we stood on the sand around Gerald Godzen, who spoke to us about the meaning of baptism. Then Gerald, with one of the leaders, waded out through the surf, until they were waist deep in the water. One by one, the new Christians made their declaration of faith, then waded out to join Gerald. They heard the words, 'I baptise you in the name of the Father, the Son and the Holy Spirit', as they were lowered gently beneath the surface to signify that their old life was dead, and then back to the light, as a sign that they now shared the risen life of Jesus. They had given a very public testimony to their new faith both to the church and to the world. Quite what the curious, end-of-season holiday-makers made of these strange goings on, I did not know. But they must have wondered what could have drawn people of all ages to participate together, because among those baptised were an 83 year-old grandmother, who was followed into the water by her daughter and grand-daughter.

During my time in the Philippines, I was led by the Holy Spirit into a consideration of the events surrounding the second coming of Jesus, as foretold in the Bible. He guided me from one Scripture to another, principally in Daniel, Ezekiel, Matthew, Thessalonians and, of course, Revelation. I did not have any reference books and indeed I was unaware that from the beginning of the Christian era right up to the present time innumerable writers had struggled to extract a coherent account from the prophecies. What I received was a sense that the return of Jesus was going to happen in the lifetime of people now born, and that Christians everywhere in the world were going to be severely persecuted immediately before His return. When I began to share this message in the Philippines, I made myself unpopular and shrank from delivering it, though my intention was not to scare people but to urge them to prepare for those days by coming to know God as their all-sufficient Provider today. But God called me back to it with great urgency to give this message to the church, and I had preached it again.

I had known that the message was not for the Philippines alone, and I had been aware for some time that I had to deliver it in Devon. I wanted to give an opportunity for as

many as wished to hear it to attend. As I prayed about it
with Gerald and members of the fellowship, we agreed
that we should hire a large hall in Paignton and advertise
it widely. The date we had arranged came a week after the
baptisms. As I remembered the resistance which the
message had encountered in the Philippines and now the
stir which the baptisms had provoked, I knew that there
would be a reaction against the message and against me.
After all, the authority of Scripture and the baptism of
believers were fairly straightforward points compared with
warning Christians about the 'mark of the Beast'. Maybe I
ought to have my bags packed ready to go immediately
after the meeting! The day before the meeting I was full of
foreboding; again, I began to listen to the devil's 'darts' of
unbelief, fear and doubt. The Lord dealt with me rather
sternly. I opened my Living Bible at Jeremiah and these
words immediately drew my attention:

> The Lord replies, stop this foolishness and talk some
> sense. Only if you return to trusting me will I let you
> continue as my spokesman. You are to influence them,
> not let them influence you. They will fight against you
> like a besieging army against a high city wall. But they
> will not conquer you for I am with you to protect and
> deliver you, says the Lord.
>
> (Jer. 15:19–20)

That rebuke from my Captain stiffened my resolve to get
back into the spiritual battle; I took authority over the
powers of darkness that were oppressing me, and praised
the Lord for His promise that He would protect me. I was
going to need it more than I knew. Up to that moment I
had been concerned about human opposition, but I was
soon to be forcibly reminded of Paul's warning that
Christians are not wrestling against flesh and blood but

against the rulers of darkness of this world.

When I woke up the next morning, I found my body covered with a rash, which was particularly bad on my hands. As I looked at them, I was thinking, 'You have a highly infectious disease; if you lay hands on the sick tonight you will pass on the infection'. I rebuked these lies from the devil and told him there was nothing he could do to stop God's word about the End-times going out tonight.

I was staying, as I always did on my visits to Paignton, with Mary and Cyril Biggs. I had settled in their sitting room, with my Bible on my lap looking up the Scripture references, which I would be using at the meeting. Through the open door I heard Mary go into the kitchen and the sounds that meant she was beginning to prepare lunch. I lifted my head and called to her, 'Don't include me in lunch, Mary, I'm fasting today'. The sparkling waters of the bay, spread out below the house, caught my eye. The splendid view from the sitting room window, normally brought a sense of wellbeing, of peace. But today, the mid-day sun reflecting from a million ripples, flickered in a restless dance; like the gleaming spearpoints of the demonic host as they wheeled and probed, looking for a chink in the armour.

The most dreadful feeling came upon me. I was conscious of the colour draining from my face. My heart was beating irregularly. Then I was gasping for breath and it felt as though everything inside my body had stopped functioning. I was aware that my heart was no longer beating. After about thirty seconds it fluttered into life. Then it stopped again. Then fluttered again. At some point I must have cried out because Mary and Cyril dashed into the room. I did not try to speak, but they were in no doubt that something very serious was happening. They began to pray in tongues. I saw a mental picture of myself being carried to an ambulance and whisked off to hospital, to be treated for a heart attack. I recognised that it was another attempt by the enemy to prevent my speaking. As Mary and Cyril prayed, the symptoms slowly passed. I rested quietly for about half an hour in the chair where I had been sitting, when, without warning my heart stopped again. At intervals, it fluttered back into action, sufficient to keep me alive, while all the time Cyril and Mary continued to pray. The symptoms passed for the second time. Before the end of the afternoon this pattern had been repeated twice more. I was however determined to speak at the meeting and forced myself to go to my room to get ready.

When I arrived at the hall, Gerald and the musicians, who were to lead the worship, were already there. When they heard what was happening to me, they gathered round to pray, sharing with me in the spiritual battle. In the first part of the meeting, I was able to take a back seat on the stage while everybody joined in the singing. I was conscious that my heart beat was still irregular and my breathing laboured, that my hands were plastered with make-up to disguise the rash and that I was making a futile attempt to look as if all was well. My time came to speak. I walked slowly to the microphone, took as deep a breath as I could manage and started. The moment I began to speak forth the word of God to His people, the miracle we had prayed for all afternoon happened. I experienced total relief from all the symptoms as though they had never been, and continued speaking for the next hour to deliver the full message I had been given. After speaking, I did, as usual, invite the sick to come for prayer and as I laid hands on them, in the name of Jesus, many were healed that night. We arrived home from the meeting tired but rejoicing. I paused just long enough on the way to bed, to wash off the make-up. It did not matter that the ugly rash was still there, I was full of thankfulness to Jesus for the way He had brought me through and the things He had done at the meeting. As I relaxed, I found myself expressing that thanks in words and then I was emboldened to ask 'Why, Lord? Why did it happen? Have I done or said something which is displeasing you?'. As had happened a number of times before, a Scripture reference came into my mind, 1 Peter 1:4–7. My Living Bible was on my bedside table; I found the place and read:

God has reserved for His children the priceless gift of eternal life, it is kept in heaven for you, pure and undefiled, beyond the reach of change and decay. And God in His mighty power will make sure that you get there safely to receive it, because you are trusting in Him. It will be yours on the last day for all to see. So be truly glad, there is wonderful joy ahead, even though the going is rough for a while down here. These trials are only to test your faith, to see whether or not it is strong and pure. It is being tested as fire tests gold and purifies it – and your faith is far more precious to God than mere gold. So if your faith remains strong after being tried in the test tube of fiery trials, it will bring you much praise and glory and honour on the day of His return.

I had just been speaking about the events preceding the 'day of His return' and of the way the faith of His people would be tested as never before. I had urged Christians to be determined about trusting the Lord for deliverance in today's trials so that they would be able to trust in the more stringent tribulation that was to come. Was the Lord saying that what I had experienced was part of my personal preparation? As He had brought me through today I was now even more assured that He would bring me through tomorrow. I snuggled down and praised Him for His faithfulness and for His priceless gift.

Chapter Four

Throughout my time in Devon, God had touched many people in a miraculous way and any single one of these was a good and sufficient reason for my having come. But in addition to these, I believe He brought me to a quiet home where I could write a book. In fact I lived in two peaceful homes; at first with Tina and Geoffrey and later with Peggy Noyce in the little village of Frogmore.

The thought of writing a book had not occurred to me. I had no natural talent of that kind and I had never been a bookish person, preferring always to do, than to read about doing. A few people had said, in a conversational way, 'You ought to write a book m'dear, it'd be more exciting than a lot I've read.' But I did not take that very seriously. It was a different matter though when, soon after I arrived in Devon, I was approached at the end of a meeting by a man who introduced himself as a publisher of Christian books. 'You have a very exciting and encouraging story to tell', he said 'and I must congratulate you on how you delivered it this evening. I'm sure it would make a good book; would you consider writing it and allowing us to publish it?' My natural reaction was to say no, but there was an excitement in my spirit that suggested that God wanted me to say yes. 'Well', I said, 'I've never tried to do anything like that before, I wouldn't know how to begin'. 'That's easily taken care of', he said, demolishing my delaying tactics, 'many people in your position haven't the time or the facility to write a perfect book but have a wonderful story in their heads. If you say yes, I will introduce you to a lady who will help you. Your part will be to write down the story as you have been telling it at meetings, with as much detail as you can remember, and she will rewrite it into book form. Will you do it?'. I did not say yes immediately, I knew it was going to take a lot of time and I wanted to be sure that it was what the Lord wanted. That night I prayed and received an inner assurance that it was God's will and a peace about what had been proposed. When I got in touch and confirmed that I was ready to go ahead he lost no time and a few days later a man from the company drove me up to Leicestershire to meet Lucy Elphinstone. As soon as I was introduced I knew that this was a divine appointment. Lucy, dark, slim and recently married to Charles, was quite different to me in so many ways. I was quickly aware of her ability to communicate and of her wide vocabulary and so was not surprised to find she had a degree in English. But when we prayed together and shared fellowship as I told her some of my adventures, we found a rapport in the Spirit which had nothing to do with academic or social background. Later on, I was to find that in some ways we were alike in temperament, in our directness and unwillingness to compromise, which occasionally led to some very healthy discussion! We arranged that I should return to Devon and start writing and send the manuscript to the publishers who would review it and send a copy to Lucy. I would then visit Lucy and spend a few days with her answering all the questions she would have after reading it. Before we left, I laid hands on her and asked the Lord that His anointing would be on every word she wrote and that He would use the book for His glory.

So, I returned to the South Hams and, in between the meetings, began to write. It took me three months of sifting through my memory, writing and rewriting to produce an accurate record of what had been the most exciting year of my life. Mindful of the Lord's word to me that I should 'give the End-time message to the church', I wrote this down too and included it as an appendix to the story of my travels. Eventually, and it seemed like an age, the manuscript was finished, parcelled up and delivered to the publishers. With a sigh of relief, feeling like a child let out of school I waited to hear from them before arranging to see Lucy again. The glow of achievement was rudely dispelled. The publishers' office telephoned me. A man's voice boomed in my ear, 'We've decided not to publish your book and will be returning your manuscript'. He did not express any regret or apologise or offer any explanation. I was so dumbfounded that I could only say, 'I will phone you tomorrow', and end the conversation. I broke the news to Peggy, who had all along encouraged me in the writing and was almost as deeply committed to the book as I was. We sat in silence, both wondering why this had happened, when God's leading had been so clear. A copy had gone to Lucy and she would already have started work on it. It was going to be a great disappointment for her, too. I wondered how to break the news to her, and what it would do to our new relationship. 'Do you think I may have offended them in some way', I asked Peggy, 'Or perhaps it was so badly written that they may have thought Lucy could do nothing with it. Did I write something which was terribly wrong or . . . ?' The questions poured out and soon we found the conversation going round in circles and ourselves becoming more and more confused. So we prayed together. As we did, a prophetic word came to me. 'Wait, do not be hasty; it is not by might nor by power but by my Spirit, says the Lord.' I did not have to sort it out, or work out a strategy to persuade the publisher to change his mind; the Lord would do all that was necessary. So I prayed, 'Lord, I will not even telephone Lucy to tell her. If it is your will that she should know please touch her heart so that she contacts me.'

The following day, I telephoned the publisher and asked for the director who had been my first contact. He, it turned out, was on a plane to Canada. I was put through, instead, to the man I had spoken to the previous day. When he came on the phone, I asked 'Why have you suddenly decided not to publish my book?' 'It's inconsistent', he replied. 'How do you mean inconsistent? I don't understand', I asked in some perplexity. 'Well,' he said, and hesitated before plunging on, 'our directors considered it yesterday and they decided it was inconsistent and they therefore could not publish it. They have made up their minds and there is really nothing more to say.' He would not be drawn further, and clearly wanted to end the conversation.

I felt hurt. I could never remember receiving such brusque treatment from a business associate when I worked in insurance. Was what I had written so terrible, I wondered. Had I failed somewhere along the line? I was tired, exhausted by the continuing spiritual battle in meetings and in long nights of ministry to the sick and the oppressed, in writing, and with all that got in the way as I followed the leading of the Spirit. The old temptation returned; 'Give it all up, go back to your job, have free time and please yourself how you spend it'. In spite of having received God's promise the day before, I found that I was descending into self-pity. I shut myself in my bedroom and poured out my frustration and weariness to the Lord.

In answer to my questioning, the Lord led me to open my Bible. It opened at Chapter eleven of Second Corinthians. I read that Paul had been lashed with a total of one hundred and ninety five stripes as well as being beaten with rods and even stoned, for proclaiming the word of God without compromise. I read on, and saw that Paul gloried in his tribulation and persecution, for in them he was made strong, for the power of Christ rested on him. I was aware of the Holy Spirit speaking to my spirit, 'Why are you sitting here, feeling sorry for yourself, bathing in self pity? Are you willing to pay the price? Don't you know that you are blessed when you are reviled and persecuted for my name's sake? Be glad. Be happy. For great is your reward in heaven. Remember, so persecuted they the prophets which were before you. Love your enemies, bless them that curse you, do good to them that hate you, and pray for those who despitefully use you and persecute you.'

The thought that there was a price to pay was not new to me; but when opposition came where I had expected support I found that the emotional cost was more than I could pay. As I let these words sink in, I saw that my heavenly Father was showing me His way through the hurt and confusion, so that it would not only be removed but replaced by gladness at what had occurred. So I got on my knees before Him and brought the names of the Board members and everyone else involved, before His throne and forgave them in Jesus' name, and asked the Lord to bless them. I said, 'Lord, I hand the publication of this book into your hands; I will do nothing more about it. If it is your will that this book be published, then I know that you will bring it to pass'. These words came from my heart, and as I spoke them, I found my mind filling up with the memories of many wonderful ways in which the Lord had worked in my life. An overwhelming sense of His faithfulness and love blotted out all my negative emotions and I found myself worshipping and praising Him who is surely worthy to be praised.

Just seven days later I had a letter from Lucy. She had bypassed the publishers and written directly to me, because she had heard nothing further. She too had been through a frustrating time. The publishers had sent her a photocopy of the manuscript, which had become undone in the post, so that it arrived with the page order totally muddled and, horror of horrors, the photocopier had missed out the page numbers. She had patiently sorted out the page order and had begun to write. I telephoned her and broke the news that I no longer had a publisher but she was not dismayed by that and wanted to carry on writing. We prayed together, in agreement, on the phone, that the Lord would find us another publisher.

The answer to that prayer lay, unknown to me in another place, and the Lord was intent on moving me there. I could see that my part in writing the book was over and I had spoken in most of the towns and villages of the South Hams, so, to that extent, I could tell myself that I had completed what the Lord had called me there to do. But I had made many friends, and some of them had become very close and dear to me. Part of me wanted to stay and this was reinforced by a request from a group who wanted me to stay and minister to them on a long-term basis. The Lord, however, was saying 'Go'.

I already knew where I should go next. Margaret and Bill Lubbock had decided on Devon for their summer holiday and called on their old friends Peter and Dianne Clarke in Kingsbridge, who had been to a number of meetings where I had spoken. Margaret and Bill were interested in what they heard God was doing and the upshot was that Margaret came to visit Peggy and me. We quickly became friends and Margaret asked me to come and visit her at Walton-on-Thames.

For several days I had been visiting friends and saying goodbyes all over the district. It had left me quiet and heavy-hearted, especially at the thought of leaving Peggy and her family of which I now felt myself to be a part. At breakfast, on the day before I was to leave, I was trying to express this to Peggy. The excitement that I could see in her eyes was strangely at odds with how I felt. She let me go on for a little while, then, with a big smile came and hugged me and said, 'Come outside, I want to show you something'. She opened the front door and almost pushed me through. There, standing in the drive, was a sparkling, bright red, new Mini. 'It's yours, Isabel', she said, 'The Lord told me to buy it for you. Alex and Rene Joy and Mary Rogers helped towards the cost'. I stood there, open mouthed, overcome by the mixed emotions of departure, and joy at the love behind this gift and the happiness at receiving such a wonderful present. I just threw my arms around her and we rejoiced together, praising the Lord. So, next morning, instead of being driven to the bus station, I loaded my suitcases now grown to two, into my brand new Mini and set off for Walton-on-Thames.

Navigation was never my strong point, so it was just as well that Margaret had given me precise directions for the journey because all the way I was full of the joy of the Lord, praising Him for taking care of me and providing for my needs. Over dinner that evening, the conversation turned to my book. 'When I visited you at Peggy's in the summer, you had nearly finished writing', said Margaret, 'When's it going to be published?' 'My publisher has turned it down', I replied, 'but Lucy is pressing on with the writing'. 'Well', she persisted, 'What are you doing about finding another publisher?' She was surprised when I said 'Not a thing', so I explained, 'God has said that He will do it by His Spirit and that it's not up to me.' She stared at me in a thoughtful silence for some moments, then said, 'I don't believe in coincidences; it just happens that my daughter Joanne's best friend's father is a director of Christian books for a major publisher. I must pray about this'. She did, and the outcome was that she introduced me to the director and his wife and we spent a pleasant evening together. I told him about some of my experiences and how I came to be looking for a publisher. He asked me to submit the manuscript to his company and he promised that one of his editors would read it quickly and give me a decision. I had it ready and there and then he took it away. He moved quickly and soon the envelope, with the company logo dropped through the letter box. I opened it eagerly and found myself facing a choice. They would, they said, be very happy to publish the testimony part of the book but they felt they ought to omit the End-time message, which I had written as an appendix. I could see that from straight commercial logic they were right; the appendix would increase the cost of producing the book without increasing the number sold and it was also likely to be controversial, and could even reduce sales. However, I believed that the Lord wanted the End-time message to be given to the church and so I asked Him what I should say in reply to the publishers' offer. I immediately knew in my spirit that it was His will to include the appendix. (I also knew that He would undertake that the publisher would not lose by including it.) So I wrote a reply, simply saying that if I consented to the book being published without the appendix, I would be disobeying the Lord and I could not do that. As I sealed the envelope, it suddenly struck me what an odd business letter this was; I wondered how I would have reacted when I was in business, if someone had written to me like that. It made me realise how much the Lord had changed me so that what He willed, not only settled what I willed to do, but provided all the reason necessary for making any decision. Three weeks later, the reply came. They would publish the whole book, which they believed would sell many copies and influence many lives. So without any 'power' or 'might' on my part the Lord had placed the book with a very big publisher which would ensure effective national distribution.

Chapter Five

'The Full Gospel Businessmen's Fellowship International warmly invites you to dinner', 'The Speaker will be Miss Isabel Chapman'. I looked at the neatly printed invitation and wondered, 'Could it have been only three years since I had gone to a meeting like this as a reluctant guest and heard a man testify how his life had been changed when he turned to Jesus?' I did not now remember much of what he said but through that testimony the Holy Spirit drew me to Jesus. Now my experience was to come full circle and people who needed to meet Jesus would be coming to hear my testimony.

This turned out to be the first of many such invitations and as the men in the Fellowship got to know me, they would arrange meetings for me in churches and public halls, so that I could speak to large numbers. This was the Lord's doing; the Fellowship does not normally have women speakers because its basic intent is that business men should hear about Jesus through the testimony of men like themselves. The love I had for the Fellowship, and my debt to them, was now increased by the opportunities they made for me to speak. For these meetings, I travelled to the four corners of the country and spoke to thousands of people. And as I ministered with the men of the fellowship, we saw hundreds come to know Jesus. Since the meetings were attended by people from all denominations I began to receive invitations to speak in churches and home fellowships. It was clear now that the gift of the Mini was God's way of saying that my settled life in Devon was at an end and the next phase of my ministry would be on the move.

However, God did not leave me without a base. Back at that same wedding in Norwich that brought me to Devon, another of the guests sought me out and said 'I am Mary Purcell and I have been wanting to meet you for months'. She told me about her home and family and invited me to call and see her in the North West and said that she wanted to invite people to her home to hear my testimony. At that time, the Lord took me off to Devon instead and it was later the following · summer that Mary, on holiday with her husband Dick, found me again and this time I fixed a date, when I would visit them. The house to which they moved soon after was close to the M6 and M62 motorways and, following that first visit, I found myself returning again and again. Mary did not mind if I arrived in the middle of the night, nor if after a long series of meetings elsewhere, I just wanted to sleep till lunch time. It was home and I could do my own thing. There were days when Mary and I would pray in the Spirit for hours, in preparation for meetings and when I was making decisions about the future direction of the ministry. It was also the place where I could catch up with the routine things that got left as I hurried from one meeting to another, like having the car serviced, getting my dry cleaning done, washing and ironing, and shopping.

I remember one evening they invited members of a church housegroup along and suggested that the members bring some friends. About fifteen people arrived and they asked me to talk about my time in the Philippines. At the end, I prayed for some who wanted to repent and accept Jesus as their Lord. One woman, who had never heard the Gospel set out clearly before, came forward, repented and accepted Jesus as Lord of her life. When I asked if she wanted Jesus to baptise her in the Holy Spirit, she wanted that too. As I prayed the power of God touched her and she fell on the floor. She lay, for a few minutes, with some of the others who had also been prayed with, and fallen. The rest of us began to sing a chorus. She got up quietly and went back to her place with a look of radiant joy on her face. She joined in the singing. A few moments later, Dick sitting near her, heard her exclaim 'I can breathe!' When the singing stopped, he asked her to explain. Since childhood, and she was now in her early forties, she had suffered from asthma and could not sing without getting out of breath. Now she realised that she was singing without effort. She had been healed as she was filled with the Spirit. I have seen other examples of people being healed without apparently asking for it. After a service in a Pentecostal church in Manchester, I was praying for a line of mainly elderly people. Many of the congregation had already left but sitting in the third row from the front, was a family with a boy of about nine years old. He suddenly took off his thick spectacles and said 'I can see, I can see the writing at the back of the platform'. He had been very short sighted and I had earlier in my testimony mentioned that my sight defect had been healed so that I could now read without glasses. Later during the ministry, he realised he could not see very well with his glasses on, took them off and found he could read the text written on the wall of the church. I was always glad when attention was directed away from me towards the Lord, especially when I spoke about healing. I wanted individual Christians to trust God for all their needs and especially for their health.

I had no contacts in Wales at this time, apart from two young teachers who asked me to come and visit them in Anglesey. Anne was the granddaughter in the family trio who were baptised in Paignton and her friend Julie had also been born again at about that time. I went, not really knowing why I was going, except that the Lord did not place any constraints when I prayed. When I arrived they told me that they had tried to arrange an opportunity for me to speak at the church they attended, but their pastor was unhappy to do that, without meeting me.

When we had caught up with each other's news and had settled down in their sitting room I explained to them that God had recently been speaking to me specifically about spending much more time praying in the Spirit, and by that He meant at least an hour a day. The passage in His Word to which He kept calling my attention says that with our natural minds, we do not know how to pray as we ought. We read together:

> Likewise the Spirit also helpeth our infirmities; for we know not what we should pray for as we ought; but the Spirit himself maketh intercession for us with groanings that cannot be uttered.
>
> Rom. 8:26, 27

This was clarified by another two verses:

> For if I pray in an unknown tongue, my Spirit prayeth, but my understanding is unfruitful
>
> 1 Cor. 14:14

> For he that speaketh in an unknown tongue, speaketh not unto men but unto God; for no man understandeth him; howbeit in the Spirit he speaketh mysteries
>
> 1 Cor. 14:2

So even though we do not know what the words mean that we are praying, God both gives them and understands them and wants them spoken on earth, to bring His will into being. Another aspect of this kind of praying is that the resistance to God's will being done on earth does not come merely from human agencies but from Satan and his princes. We looked together at Ephesians 6.

> For we are not fighting against people made of flesh and blood, but against persons without bodies – the evil rulers of the unseen world, those mighty satanic beings and great evil princes of darkness who rule this world; and against huge numbers of wicked spirits in the spirit world!
>
> Eph. 6:12 (LB)

They had both been baptised in the Spirit and had the ability to speak in tongues, so they understood what I meant. Talking to them helped me, too, because it gave me the opportunity to put into words what the Holy Spirit had been putting into my mind as I meditated on it.

I have heard preachers, when teaching on the gifts of the Spirit, trying to rank them in order of importance and they generally put speaking in an unknown tongue at the bottom of the list. But Paul said 'Now concerning spiritual gifts brethren, I would not have you ignorant. Now there are diversities of gifts, but the same Spirit. And there are differences of administrations, but the same Lord. And there are diversities of operations, but it is the same God which worketh all in all.

BUT THE MANIFESTATION OF THE SPIRIT IS GIVEN TO EVERY MAN TO PROFIT WITHAL.'
(1 Cor. 12:1, 4–7)

There is no doubt that the manifestation of the Spirit on the day of Pentecost was that they ALL spoke in tongues, and the gift of tongues is available today for every believer who will receive it by faith.

Paul then goes on to explain about the other gifts of the

Spirit. In my own experience, the gift of speaking in tongues has been made manifest almost every time I prayed for a believer to receive the baptism in the Holy Spirit. This suggested to me that God had designed it to have a fundamental usefulness in the life of the Christian. This was reinforced when I read Paul's comment to the church at Corinth, whose members certainly did not undervalue the gift, that

I speak with tongues more than you all!

1 Cor. 14:18

It was clear from this whole chapter that Paul regarded the private and public speaking as distinct manifestations of the gift, for the individual; speaking in tongues 'edified himself', which means built up his spiritual life, and enabled him to pray as he ought. As we pray in the Spirit we are pulling down Satan's strongholds and opening up the way, for God's perfect will to be done.

As we talked about it, and read the Scriptures, I became more than ever convinced that this was what God wanted me to do, and a great sense that the period immediately ahead required it. When I said I wanted to start right away, they asked me if they could join in and we began. The result of that first one hour session produced an extra-ordinary response in Anne and Julie. They both became much more open to the Lord's leading and became convinced that they should immediately do two things, destroy their records of rock music and pour away their stock of homemade wine. I had not said anything to them on either subject, it was entirely in response to God's convincing them that they needed to be free of both. About fifty records were destroyed and several gallons of wine were poured down the drain. They told me that, before they were born again, they would often drink too much and it usually led to trouble. I prayed for them and they were set free, and delivered, through the power in the name of Jesus.

I went to see their pastor and he invited me to speak. People at that little meeting, who saw God's power in evidence, talked about it and I began to receive other invitations to speak. Every day, we prayed at home together, in the Spirit, for more than an hour, sometimes several times a day. The meetings grew in size and in demonstration of God's power. During the fortnight that I stayed with Julie and Anne, the Lord arranged a meeting for me every night. In an area stretching from Holyhead to Colwyn Bay, we experienced the Lord pouring out his Spirit in Wales. I believe that the effectiveness of those meetings, owed much to our prayers in the Spirit, which had broken through the defences of the demonic powers and compelled them to release people to receive the truth of the Gospel of Jesus.

On that last Sunday morning in Wales, I sat on the platform of a church in Colwyn Bay quietly praying, waiting for the service to start. As Pastor John Thorngate rose promptly at ten thirty to welcome his congregation, there was no tangible evidence that this was going to be any different from all the Sundays before. The Word was read, hymns were sung and I was introduced. As I went to the lectern, I was conscious that the anointing of the Holy Spirit which had increased from meeting to meeting was greater than ever. I felt a great freedom to speak out, with directness and without ambiguity. What the Holy Spirit was doing in my mouth he began to do in the hearts of the people and as I looked around their faces I could see that they were receiving what they were hearing. There was a slight disturbance in the centre aisle. As I watched, a lady wearing a surgical collar, under the power of the Spirit, slipped from her seat and lay in the aisle. I continued to speak for the next half an hour, while she lay quite still. I asked people who had needs to come forward but the Holy Spirit was already doing His work and people were receiving ministry from Him where they sat, some sliding on to the floor as His power touched them, some breaking out in tongues as Jesus baptised them in the Spirit. Some were praying earnestly and repenting and making Jesus Lord of their lives.

A ten-year-old girl came shyly to the front; she told me she could not hear in her right ear. I commanded the ear to open in the name of Jesus. When I tested with a whisper and it was clear to the watching congregation that she could hear, their eyes filled with tears as they recognised God's love and power at work. Her name was Sarah Lee and she wrote about it afterwards

When I was born ten years ago, I was deaf in my right ear. Not being able to hear properly has caused a lot of problems. At school I was frightened. I could not hear the teacher, and got into trouble. One Sunday a lady came to our church, and told us how God had worked among the headhunters of the Philippine Islands, healing their diseases. During the meeting I went forward and asked her to pray and ask Jesus to heal me. At first there was pain in my deaf ear, then suddenly I could hear a little bit. Gradually my hearing got better and better.

As this was going on, the lady with the surgical collar stood up, removed the collar and began to bend, stretch and leap about. She told me afterwards that she had arthritis in her spine and the bones were 'crumbling' and she was in constant pain. She had felt warmth all over her body and had not been very conscious of what was going on in the meeting but she knew something very powerful was happening to her back. When she got up, she found all the pain had gone and full mobility had returned. Jesus had miraculously healed her.

Many other people were healed and it was one of those occasions when no one wanted to leave, though by now the service had long overrun its usual finishing time. The presence of the Holy Spirit was so warm and secure that for me and I think everyone else there, it was the most wonderful place we could be. Someone started to sing and we spent the next hour and a half praising and thanking God, for who He was and for what He had done that day.

Chapter Six

Christmas was coming and as I drove North for my last engagement of 1984 my thoughts were turning to Scotland. Away in the North, in Aberdeenshire, my mother knew I had kept the last week of the year free to share the time with her and to give her the news of my travels and of the book, of which she was so proud. *Arise and Reap* had been in the bookshops for nearly a year. She would be anxiously awaiting news about its progress and I knew she would be delighted to hear that the first printing had sold out within a few months. When I had seen her at Easter, I had told her about a live interview with Michael Hart in Nottingham for Central TV in which I was able to give a short testimony and to pray for the sick over the air. Now I would be able to show her a letter from a lady called Doreen in Leicester who wrote,

> I was one of the people who received healing as a result of your prayer on Central TV on January 19th. The Lord very graciously healed the pain I had suffered for years in my spine, and I continue to praise Him.

My immediate destination was, however, even further away than Aberdeenshire. I had a long standing invitation from Rev. Hamish Cormach to visit Wick in the Highlands, only seventeen miles from John o'Groats. During the summer I had spoken in Cornwall and in Jersey, so this trip meant that I would have traversed the whole of the country.

As I drove on the longest journey of the year, I sang and prayed and enjoyed many hours of fellowship with Jesus. He spoke to me about the power that was available to Christians and His wish that they should use it to meet needs and demonstrate His glory. He said:

> Many hearts lie dormant, many hearts long to be aflame in my service. Call forth that flame; cause it to burn in my service. Help my people to know who they are, in me, so that miracles may be performed. Then hands, that are stretched forth in love, shall know my healing power, that my glory shall be more manifest. Show the power of my providence in your own life, despite your smallness and frailty.

The congregation at Wick turned out in force for the meetings, eager to hear what the Spirit was saying to the church and to be encouraged. They were part of the church, the bride which Jesus was preparing for Himself; a bride whom He would enable to come victoriously and gloriously through persecution. Their hearts were open to receive His power and authority and many were born again and baptised in the Holy Spirit, with the evidence of speaking in tongues.

My hostess at Wick was Miss Emma Bruce and in a letter written just after I had returned to my mother's home she said

> Only yesterday, I was stopped in the street by a young woman with a little girl of four, an adopted child who had been profoundly deaf. She was healed instantly when you prayed for her and now they are spreading the Good News and rejoicing in the Lord.

Roderick, a twelve-year-old boy, who was prone to urinary

infections throughout his childhood, had been medically diagnosed as having a congenital obstruction of his urinary tract. He was asked to write his testimony, and it was sent to me:

A woman evangelist came to our church in Wick. Her sermons were amazing and gave me knowledge of what was going to happen to those who do not know God and to Christians, when the End-times are here. It makes me so glad to be a Christian. I always read in the Bible how God heals. I thought it was only when Jesus was on earth that people were healed, but this woman said that God still heals today. Now, I happen to have had a series of operations, and I was due to go for another in five days' time. I trusted that God would heal me if Isabel prayed for me, and I accepted that, by Jesus' stripes, I was healed. So, I went out and she prayed for me, and the devil had to leave me. I praise God that I never went for that operation and never will. Any time I am attacked by disease, I rebuke the devil and he has to flee.

Even at a small town meeting, there were often thirty or forty sick people who needed prayer. I met them for such a short period, that I never knew the full extent of the pain and disablement and disruption that the devil had inflicted on individuals or the wonderful release and wholeness that Jesus brings. Claire didn't look very ill when I laid hands on her in the name of Jesus but her mother's letter afterwards showed me just how wonderful her healing was. Elizabeth Yaudie's letter said

Thought I'd better give you an outline of the problem Claire, who is now nine years old, used to have. A large lump came up on the left side of her neck in the lymph gland when she was 3 years of age. Despite many different antibiotics (13 bottles of the stuff in fact) the lump was resistant to them all. A surgeon opened the lump twice and it eventually drained over several months. Needless to say she was a very ill little girl over this period of time, she had very little energy having to be carried about.

For the following 3–4 years she was never completely well, complaining of headaches and stomach pains. This became very acute again and all her lymphatic system became active. She would lie and weep and scream as the lymph glands swelled up all over her body. The headaches and stomach pains were diagnosed as abdominal migraine and she averaged 3–4 attacks per week, lasting anything from a couple of hours to a complete day. She was prescribed tablets (Sanomigran) which she would have to take 3 times a day probably for life. The side effects gave mood changes (she changed from being a gentle loving little girl into a very unhappy, irritable stranger), kidney and liver damage etc.

It was also obvious that she had become allergic to many foods probably caused by intestinal damage due to the high dosage of antibiotics over a prolonged period. About 15–20 minutes after having food with wheat, sugar, milk, eggs or certain flavourings and colourings, Claire would be flat out on the settee, screaming with pain. Her lymph glands in her neck would swell up so much that she had no jaw line to be seen.

When we came home from the meeting in December 1984, Claire said, 'Mum, is it true that I can eat anything at all?'. Mustering up all my faith I said 'Yes you can'. So she said 'In that case I'll have a huge plate of ice cream!!' She had been unable to eat ice cream for over a year, as it had the worst reaction on her of all along with chocolate. True to her words Claire ate a soup plate full of ice cream, licked her lips and duly went to bed. Over the following day she had a diet of several plates of ice cream and all the junk food one could imagine, and some we couldn't, and she was not ill. She eats everything and has no adverse reactions. She is on no medication of any kind. For so long we wondered whether Claire was going to live, let alone live a normal life. Praise the Lord and bless you Isabel, she lives, she lives in and through our Lord Jesus.

I wept when I received this letter. They were tears of gratitude for a God who long ago had proclaimed the Christmas message of peace and good will, that His glory might be manifested in the Highest. Claire's healing was a witness to all the angelic host, to the powers and principality of darkness and to all creation that God's glory was on the earth. Thanks be to God for His inexpressible gift!

Chapter Seven

God is willing to heal everyone. I often made this statement and it was one that was frequently challenged, not only in Devon but also in most of the places where I spoke. The word of God seemed to me to be quite clear, but why then were so many believers sick? I needed to know and since those first objections after my return to England, I had been asking the Lord for His truth concerning healing. The Lord showed me in the Philippines that when I preached the word of life it would be confirmed by signs and miracles. He also required me to tell the church that each individual Christian was to look to Him for health and healing.

I prayed and fasted and over a period, the Lord drew my attention to passages of Scripture and spoke words into my spirit. Jesus compared His provision for Salvation with that for Healing.

On Salvation He said:

I so loved the world, that I gave my only begotten Son, that whosoever believes in Him shall not perish, but have everlasting life. The wages of sin is death, but the gift of God is eternal life, through Jesus my Son. I get no pleasure in any man's death; it is not my will that any man should die and go to Hell, but men are dying daily, they go to Hell daily, because they will not repent of their sins. They will not by faith receive forgiveness of their sins, through the blood of my Son, shed at Calvary, so they are going to Hell. They will be cast into the lake of fire, and there they will spend eternity in the place that was prepared for Satan and his demons. They will be separated from me and all that is good for the whole of eternity, which is a time without end, but this is not my will for any man.

On healing He said:

My Son bore your sickness, my Son carried your pains and by His stripes you are healed. My people perish through lack of knowledge, my people perish through double mindedness, my people perish through unbelief. It is written in my Word that I have given you power over all the powers of the darkness, in the name of my Son Jesus. Is it not written in my Word, resist the devil and he will flee? Is it not written that my Son already bore your sickness and carried your pains, and by His stripes you were healed? My people have many other gods before me; instead of believing my Word, instead of applying my Word to their situation and circumstances, they run to the other gods in their lives, to where their faith lies for healing. Their faith lies in the physicians of Egypt, their faith lies in the remedies of mere man, their faith lies in the arm of flesh.

But I am the Lord your God who heals you. My Son bore your sickness and carried your pains so that you do not have to and by His stripes you are healed. But who will believe my Word? Who will believe my report? My will for my children is that they live and walk in divine health and glorify me in their body, which is my temple.

I checked in Scripture that the death of Jesus redeemed us from sin and from sickness. In the Gospel accounts I read about Jesus in Gethsemane.

Then cometh Jesus with them unto a place called Gethsemane, and saith unto the disciples, Sit ye here while I go and pray yonder. And he took with Him Peter and the two sons of Zebedee and began to be very sorrowful and very heavy. Then saith He unto them, My soul is exceeding sorrowful, even unto death: tarry ye here and watch with Me. And He went a little further and fell on His face and prayed, saying, O my Father, if it be possible let this cup pass from Me: nevertheless not as I will, but as Thou wilt.

(Matt. 26:36–39)

And there appeared an angel unto Him from heaven, strengthening Him, and being in an agony He prayed more earnestly; and His sweat was as it were great drops of blood falling down to the ground.

(Luke 22:43–44)

Jesus was aware of the horrors of the hours on the cross which lay ahead of Him, yet He was willing that He should not only die, but suffer torture when He died. When the soldiers came to arrest Him He refused to allow His disciples to resist.

Thinkest thou not that I cannot now pray to my Father, and He shall presently give me more than twelve legions of angels?

(Matt. 26:53)

He had given the Father His word, 'Not my will but yours be done'. There was no other way for man to be saved, no other blood that could take away sin.

Immediately after this, He was tried and condemned to be crucified. The crucifixion was to be preceded by the terrible torture of scourging.

> And so Pilate, willing to content the people, released
> Barabbas unto them, and delivered Jesus, when he had
> scourged him, to be crucified.
>
> (Mark 15:5)

Jesus was tied to a post and beaten with a scourge. This was
not a whip. It was an instrument of torture, often used to
extract confessions from prisoners. It consisted of a number
of leather thongs into which were tied small sharp pieces of
metal. These tore through the flesh of the back and dragged
strips off the bone. It was not unusual for people to die after
scourging. Under this hideous torture our Saviour's back
was so terribly torn that no blow could possibly be dis-
tinguished from another. Every area of His back was
brutally bruised and lacerated. By the whippings and
beatings, the pain and agony of those stripes, we were
healed, if only we will believe it.

Matthew says that when Jesus healed people, He was
fulfilling the prophecy which came through Isaiah:

> He cast out the spirits with his Word, and healed all
> that were sick: that it might be fulfilled which was
> spoken by Esaias the prophet, saying, Himself took our
> infirmities, and bore our sicknesses.
>
> (Matt. 8:16–17)

He was quoting from Chapter 53 of Isaiah at verse 4, the
passage continues in verse 5:

> But he was wounded for our transgressions, he was
> bruised for our iniquities, the chastisement of our peace
> was upon him and with His stripes we are healed.

In his first epistle, Peter says of Jesus,

57

Who his own self bore our sins in his own body on the tree, that we, being dead to sins, should live unto righteousness; by whose stripes ye were healed.

(1 Pet. 2:24)

The account of the torture of Jesus continues:

Then the soldiers of the Governor took Jesus into the common hall and gathered unto him the whole band of soldiers. They stripped him and put on him a scarlet robe. And when they had plaited a crown of thorns, they put it on his head and a reed in his right hand; and they bowed the knee before him and mocked him, saying, 'Hail, King of the Jews!' And they spit upon him and took the reed and smote him on the head. And after they had mocked him they took the robe off from him and put his own raiment on him and led him away to crucify him.

(Matt. 27:27–31)

The sacrificial lamb of God lay down on the wooden cross, stretched out His arms; the huge spikes were driven through His hands and feet. They lifted up the cross and dropped it into its stand and there hung the sacrificial lamb, suspended between heaven and earth. The blood was flowing out of His back where He had been beaten and lashed. The blood was dripping down His forehead where they had thrust the crown of thorns, the blood was flowing from His hands and feet where the cruel spikes had been driven. Those standing around the cross hurled all manner of abuse at the Lord Jesus Christ. And Jesus, hanging on the cross, in excruciating pain, cried to His Father

Father, forgive them; for they know not what they do.

Luke 23:34

The bystanders were unaware that Jesus was shedding His spotless blood to pay the price of their sins. They were unaware that Jesus had allowed His body to be scourged for their physical benefit.

As Jesus hung on the cross, in the middle of the day, darkness suddenly came upon the earth from noon till three o'clock. Because of the darkness no one could see what was happening to Jesus on the cross, but the Lord God Jehovah revealed to us, through the prophet Isaiah, what did actually happen during that time of blackness.

> His visage was so marred more than any man, and His form more than the sons of men.
>
> (Isa. 52:14)

I believe that darkness came upon the earth during those three hours because man could not stand to look upon Jesus in such suffering. The things suffered by Jesus on the cross at Calvary are beyond human imagining, as He was bearing our diseases. His appearance was so disfigured that He became an object of horror. His body was marred beyond human recognition.

> Yet it was the Lord's good plan to bruise Him and fill Him with grief. But when His soul had been made an offering for sin, then He shall have a multitude of children, many heirs. He shall live again and God's programme shall prosper in His hands. And when He sees all that is accomplished by the anguish of His soul, He shall be satisfied; and because of what He has experienced, my righteous servant shall make many to be counted righteous before God, for He shall bear all their sins.
>
> Isa. 53:10-11 (LB)

Among the things which were accomplished by the anguish of

His soul was healing, as verses 4 and 5 say, Surely (certainly, undoubtedly) He (Christ) hath borne our griefs (the Hebrew word 'kholee' translated 'griefs' here, is I am told, more usually, elsewhere in the Bible, translated 'sickness') and carried our sorrows ('makob' – 'pains'). (Christ certainly bore our sickness and carried our pains.) Yet we did esteem Him smitten of God and afflicted. (They thought God was punishing Jesus because He said He was the Son of God.) But He was wounded for our transgressions (offences). He was bruised for our iniquities (wickedness), the chastisement (punishment) of our peace was upon Him, (the punishment needed to obtain peace and wellbeing for us was upon Him) and with His stripes we are healed. (With the stripes and lashes that wounded Him we are healed and made whole.)

Some religious leaders have told me, that the healing spoken of in Isaiah 53, Matthew 8 and 1 Peter 2:24 refers to spiritual healing, which takes place when a Christian goes to heaven. But Jesus said, that what qualifies us for heaven, is that we should be born again, now, on earth. Healing is for our physical bodies and it is for now. Isaiah says 'with His stripes we are healed' and 'are' is present, not future tense. Peter writing after the death of Jesus, in quoting it, puts it in the past tense to show that sickness, like sin, was dealt with once and for all by Jesus.

Sadly, Christians have been taught that, although they are redeemed from their sin, they must continue to suffer their sicknesses, because it may not be God's will to heal them. They know He healed others, but think that those who were healed were somehow more fortunate people on whom He decided to bestow mercy; as for the less fortunate, they must be patient and continue to bear the 'cross' of their physical suffering.

Before I understood these scriptures, I prayed for healing for myself and other people on the basis that our heavenly

Father hears and answers those who pray, for example according to John's Gospel:

> If ye abide in me, and my words abide in you, ye shall ask what ye will and it shall be done unto you.
>
> John 15:7

Now God was saying that healing was accomplished on the cross and was a specific scriptural promise which He had spoken in His word through Isaiah, through Matthew and through Peter and any Christian could receive it by believing the truth of His Word, and knowing that the Holy Spirit would perform it.

Another aspect of the Lord's provision for healing is that it is part of the new covenant between God and every believer. Even the old covenant between God and the Jewish nation promised healing.

> Wherefore it shall come to pass, if ye hearken to these judgments, and keep, and do them, that the Lord thy God shall keep unto thee the covenant and the mercy which he sware unto thy fathers
>
> (Deut. 7:12)

> . . . the Lord will take away from thee all sickness, and will put none of the evil diseases of Egypt, which thou knowest, upon thee.
>
> (Deut. 7:15)

The new covenant between God and all who believe in Jesus is a better covenant than the old one.

> He (Jesus) is the mediator of a better covenant which was established upon better promises.
>
> (Heb. 8:6)

This new covenant is celebrated every time believers receive the bread and wine in the service which is called in various churches Communion, or Eucharist, or Lord's Supper or simply Breaking of Bread. Paul, in his letter to the first-century Christians at Corinth reminded them of the significance of the bread and wine:

> the Lord Jesus the same night in which he was betrayed took bread: and when he had given thanks, he brake it, and said, Take eat: this is my body, which is broken for you: this do in remembrance of me. After the same manner also he took the cup, when he had supped, saying, This cup is the new testament (covenant) in my blood: this do ye, as oft as ye drink it, in remembrance of me.
>
> (1 Cor. 11:23–25)

Paul then went on to say:

> He that eateth and drinketh unworthily, eateth and drinketh judgement to himself, not discerning the Lord's body. For this cause many are weak and sickly among you, and many sleep.
>
> (1 Cor. 11:28–29)

Paul was here teaching the Corinthians that they were sick and weak and even dying before their time because they did not believe or understand that the body of the Lord Jesus was broken, beaten, lashed, marred and twisted for their physical benefit. They did not believe in the sacrifice of the scourging of Jesus to heal their bodies. They were partaking of the bread without believing God's word and as they did not trust the Lord's word the blessings of the everlasting covenant were withheld from them. So they continued to bring judgement on themselves, in that they were still sick and many even died before their time. Sadly the same thing is true today; Isaiah's cry comes down the centuries 'Who will believe our report?'

Joan Cowan was healed, not because I prayed for her, but because she came into an understanding of all that Jesus had done for her by His suffering and death and she responded to it. On a day when the pain was particularly bad, she was brought, in her wheelchair, to the Wings of Peace camp in Cornwall, where Pastor Richard Uglow had invited me to come and speak. The Holy Spirit moved mightily and Joan was healed. This is her own account of what happened.

In ignorance I accepted Satan's 'gift' of Multiple Sclerosis two years ago. I presumed God had allowed it to happen. It was such a joy to be in the company of people in the same frame of mind as myself. I had had such a bad day with so much pain and weakness that it helped to take my mind off it. I knew the Holy Spirit prompted me to go forward when you offered healing in Jesus' name, but I have to admit I was thinking, well Lord, you have a tough one here. O me of little faith, nothing is impossible for God to do, and I rebuked the devil for putting such a thought into my head. Whilst you were ministering to the other folk, I was praying quietly in tongues, and suddenly I had a picture of Jesus on the cross. Not as I had always imagined before – the perfect body, albeit with a sad face, with the white loin cloth – but my picture was of the most brutally beaten bruised, twisted, grotesque body I had ever seen. I wanted to cry. Then you whispered in my ear, change your doctor. Dr. Jesus will heal you, and again I saw Him hanging there on that cross, suffering for me, so that I might be free of the bondage of that wheelchair. What a price to be paid. Thank you Jesus. I remember you holding my hands and praying in the Spirit, and my legs suddenly felt so strong. Whilst I was always able to walk a few yards with a stick, I could not stand unaided, and yet there I was standing, and then the power of God surged through every part of me, repairing, renewing and strengthening my weary frame. I shook, but I was not afraid, nor was it painful. As the shaking subsided I felt completely at peace. Standing unaided, I remember walking, upright and strong, back to my husband, who had tears in his eyes. My son was totally nonplussed by it all. Then I saw a friend; I wanted to hug her so I walked over to her and said, 'I could run a mile'. 'Come on then', she replied, and off we went. I had not run for over two years, but instantly by God's gracious healing power my muscles all worked and I could run. Praise God, Hallelujah! Three weeks later my husband responded to an altar call and gave his heart to the Lord Jesus. I have signed off the sick list and the Occupational Therapists' list and on to the dole. I know God will provide for the income we have lost, now that I have returned all my disabled person's benefit books. My life now belongs to Him completely and even though many folks have laughed in my face when I tell them, like you I just say, 'Father forgive them, they just do not know'.

Four months later I received a letter from Joan saying that the Lord had provided a job for her; she wrote:

I am now working in a very demanding job as a personal secretary for a lawyer, plus doing voluntary work and running my home.

Like the woman who pressed through the throng to touch the hem of Jesus' garment and knew in herself that she was healed, Gwyneth knew that Jesus was willing to heal her. She wrote very briefly from her home in Newport:

The week before you came to minister at the Full Gospel Businessmen's Fellowship dinner, I had suffered a haemorrhage from my back passage. My doctor examined me and said he felt a lump and told me I would have to see a surgical consultant. Just before I was due to see the consultant I attended the meeting, the power of God came upon me and I fell to the ground. I knew that Jesus had healed me. Two days later the consultant examined me and there was no growth there. Praise the Lord.

With a very small child there is no possibility of its participating, but God heals on the basis of an adult Christian believing for them. This was the case with Rebekah; her parents Rosemary and Alan wrote to me from Cheltenham, where I had been speaking, and said:

Rebekah at the age of eight months became very ill with a condition called osteomyelitis, which is a form of septic arthritis, in her left ankle. She was admitted to hospital and immediately operated on. Apparently the chances of developing this condition are literally millions to one. For nearly two years she was in great pain, she walked with a limp and we were told to expect further operations when she was four years old. I brought Rebekah along to the Elim Church, where you sat her on your lap, cuddled her and prayed for her. Immediately we noticed a remarkable difference in the way she walked, her limp disappeared completely and the purple bruising on her ankle joint disappeared also. In November when she returned to the hospital for further X-rays and check-ups, the consultant could not believe his eyes when comparing the two sets of X-rays from earlier in the year. Although her bones creaked slightly, he said the bone restoration was such as he had hoped to achieve by further operations as she grew older. He was amazed at the way she walked and ran, he said it was so incredible that he would take her X-rays to a conference for discussion. Hallelujah! Rebekah tells people that she sat on your lap and she talked to Jesus and He made her foot better.

I met Karen and her parents, when I visited South Wales and she came to a meeting where I was speaking. She believed when she came, that God could heal her, at the meeting, she realised that He would. This is how a reporter told the story after interviewing Karen and her father:

Do you believe in miracles? Schoolgirl Karen Edwards and her family do. Karen at the age of fifteen developed lumps under her arms. Within a month they spread to her neck, and tests showed that she had Hodgkin's Disease, a lymph gland cancer. She had major surgery to remove her spleen and had begun radiotherapy. Then she went with her parents, who are born-again Christians, to a Christian holiday camp, near Newtown. Karen joined deaf, blind and arthritic people who went forward for prayer, and saw an amazing transformation in them. 'I saw what was happening to them and thought, if God can do that for them He can do it for me', said Karen, describing how an arthritic woman shuffled up for prayer, then disregarded her walking frame as she walked back down the hall.

Her father said, 'As she was prayed for in Jesus' name, I saw a miracle happen right in front of my eyes. Karen came bounding back to her seat absolutely radiant and announced, "I am healed". Within twelve hours the lumps that had been the size of bantam's eggs had reduced to pea size and continued to do so'. Karen said, 'I feel absolutely fine, better than I have done for at least a year. I can run and jump without getting tired, and eat as much as I like'.

The following letter from a friend brought the good news that she had been healed:

I can never forget how the Lord touched me and healed my body from arthritis. I am thirty years old with a family of three children and it was whilst I was expecting my first child that my problems started. The doctor found that the body and head were rested on the pelvic bone, which put the pelvic joint out at both sides. This caused a great deal of pain which persisted with the following two children. The only treatment for this was to take painkilling tablets and make several trips to an osteopath, which did not help much. Then I had a car accident and damaged my knees and arthritis formed in both knees and pelvic joints. The pain gradually became unbearable, making bending and walking an agony. After several visits to the doctor, he referred me to a specialist, who proceeded to give me cortisone injections into the joints. This helped for a while but the effect soon wore off, and I was coming to the end of my tether with pain. Again I visited the doctor and he gave me the drug called Opren, which I found helped quite a bit. Then one day I forgot to take the pills, the next day I didn't know how to move. The pain was so bad I had to get my mother in to look after the children. Then I was invited to a house-meeting where I was told you, Isabel, were going to share your testimony. Then you got round to asking if anyone wanted prayer for healing. I sat there and said nothing. I knew the Lord could heal me but I was afraid in case it wasn't to be and I didn't want my children's faith to be damaged. Then my mother-in-law called to you and told you about me. You asked if I believed that God could heal me and I did believe, so we prayed together and asked the Lord to heal my back and legs. I tried to move afterwards and they did not feel any different to me. When I got home I thought I must have some faith, so I did not take any tablets and I knew that unless the Lord healed me I would be absolutely hopeless the next day, which was Sunday, and I had all the young people coming in for tea. So I said, 'right Lord, it's up to you'. Well I awoke in the morning and I ran down the stairs without thinking. So I thought – mmm – so I have, and I turned round and ran back up again. Then I knew the Lord had healed me. I was just so happy, I had not run up or down stairs for years, at best it was a slow dragging walk. I was so excited and I realised I had slept all night, something else I could not do before as the pain would wake me up during the night and now I was free.

I visited the area where this dear sister lived, some months later, and heard the terrible news that she had lost her healing and that all the pain was back. I telephoned her and asked if I could go and visit her, but the answer was No. I sent her the tape *By His Stripes We Are Healed*, but I don't know if she ever listened to it. My last report of her was she was still in a great deal of pain.

Why did it happen? I re-read her letter. Could it be that she did not really believe that she was healed, until she saw the evidence of it when she ran downstairs? She had no real revelation of all that Jesus had accomplished for her on the cross. Her heart was not established with the fact that 'by the Lord's stripes she was healed' and she depended on what she saw and felt. Sadly this is often the case with people who get healed through the faith of others. The devil takes advantage of their lack of understanding and brings back the symptoms, which fills them with fear and doubt. They are like the man in the parable which Jesus told, who built his house on sand: the storm came and destroyed it. The enemy will try to rob us of our healing, this is why it is vitally important that we understand the power in the name of Jesus, and resist the devil when he attacks, and stand fast on the word of God. When we come to the place of knowing, we know that 'by the Lord's stripes we are healed', the enemy will have no power over us. When the storm comes, you will simply say, 'Satan, you know you are defeated, in Jesus' name I command you to leave my body', and he must obey. Then having done all, we must stand and hold our ground.

When one part of the body is hurting, we are all hurting. It still hurts me to think of my dear sister in Christ and all the members of His body, who are suffering sickness, through a lack of understanding of all that Jesus accomplished for our physical benefit as well as our spiritual benefit. I, myself, found, one day, that I had a lump in my breast. The first thing that happened was that fear entered my mind. It was a powerful, nagging fear. It attacked me during the day and even invaded my dreams at night. Fear does not come from God. His word says specifically:

For God hath not given us the spirit of fear

2 Tim. 1:7

I knew from experience that fear was the opposite to faith and the two cannot coexist. I determined that I would put my full trust in the Word of the Lord. Since fear is from the devil, I banished the spirit of fear from my mind, in Jesus' name, and told my body to come into line with the word of God, which says that by His stripes I was healed.

This occurred soon after the Lord had shown me, through His word that He had made provision for His covenant children to live with victory over disease. The next time I attended a celebration of Communion, I lifted the cup of the covenant to my lips and asked Jesus to forgive me of my sins. I examined my heart to ensure I had no unforgiveness there, then I partook of the cup knowing that the wine of the cup represented the blood of Jesus that had been shed to cleanse me from all unrighteousness. I then partook of the bread knowing that the bread represents the body of Jesus, that was beaten and lashed for my physical benefits and by His stripes I was healed. I spoke to the forces of darkness that were attacking my body and commanded that all that was of darkness leave my body instantly in Jesus' name. I asked Jesus to let His healing power flow through me and heal me. Through faith in God's word I received my healing.

But the lump was still there and the stabbing pains were still there. For the next few days, I continued to check to see if it were better. Then I realised that checking proceeded from doubt rather than faith, so I asked the Lord to forgive me and said, 'Lord I will not be affected by what I see and feel, I will only be affected by that which is written in your Word'. Day by day, for three weeks, I stood on the Word of God. I believed that by the Lord's stripes I was healed, and as I confessed the Word of God, His Word was made manifest in my body. The lump started to get smaller and smaller, until it completely disappeared. This trial, from which the Lord delivered me, gave me great assurance in encouraging believers to see in the communion service God's covenant promises to every believer.

Chapter Eight

God had planted the seed of a desire in my heart and I watered it, at intervals, for two years in my prayers. I knew one day it would sprout and grow and I would get there, but I did not know when or how. 'There' was Israel. I had wondered about routing my journey back from the Philippines through Tel Aviv and spending a week or two in the country but, at the last moment, I had no assurance that it was God's time, so I flew straight back to England. But now something was stirring.

The time was almost right and the piece of God's complex design which included me and my desire to go to Israel was about to be executed. I had briefly met Frank Pass but that did not seem to be significant at the time. So I was surprised, when I arrived at the home of my friends Jack and Eva Logan, where I was staying while ministering in Bidford-on-Avon to hear that Frank had telephoned and asked for me. 'You'll never guess what he wants to tell you', said an excited Eva. 'Frank who?' I asked. 'Frank Pass, you remember', she said, and she was bursting to tell me so I let her go on. 'He says that the Lord woke him up last night and he heard an inner voice say that he was to finance your trip to Israel!' I was delighted. So I telephoned him and he repeated what Eva had told me. I had to explain that, though I had long known that the Lord would take me to Israel, I had no immediate plans. 'Well, let me know when you are going' was his cheerful response. With grateful thanks I rang off and began to pray. 'Thank you Lord that you have a plan for me to go to Israel, please show me when and with whom I am to go.' I was confident that the plan would soon begin to unfold. What I did not know was that God was planning through it to meet another, separate desire of my heart.

I had a fruitful and happy time of ministry around Bidford that week, with John and Eva. My next series of meetings were back in Devon. I loaded up my red Mini and set off for familiar territory. My first meeting was to be at Torbay with the fellowship group which had grown up while I was in the area before. That week, it also happened that Gerald Godzen was at home after one of his overseas evangelistic trips and his distinctive shape appeared, heading towards me as soon as I entered the hall. He greeted me, and his first question was, 'Are you coming to Jerusalem?' 'Funny you should say that Gerald,' I replied, 'because only last week, the Lord provided the finances for me to go. But why do you ask?' 'I thought you might have heard that a lot of Christians are planning to be in Jerusalem this autumn, for the Jewish Feast of Tabernacles', he replied and went on, 'I will be there, I am going with a group organised by PFI.' 'What's PFI?' I asked, wondering why Gerald should think I would know these initials. 'Prayer For Israel is a loose organisation of people from all over the country who undertake to pray regularly for the welfare of Israel and Jews everywhere. They have chartered a plane and arranged hotel accommodation and a tour of all the interesting sites. I know there are places still available! Why don't you call around tomorrow and I'll show you a video of last year's visit.' I found the film enthralling, but more than that I felt the presence, the anointing of the Holy Spirit come as I watched. I knew this was God's time and means. So I asked Gerald to book me a place and wrote and told Frank about it. He promptly provided £500, and it was settled. I had a busy summer schedule ahead of me and as I worked through it and criss-crossed the country in the Mini, I would now and again thank God for the provision of the wonderful holiday he had arranged.

Gerald took me round the departure lounge at Heathrow and introduced me to the other people on the tour. There were people from all parts of Britain, and, as I waited, I found myself sitting in the lounge next to a lady in her fifties, to whom I had just been introduced. Her name was Daphne. She was, I gathered, from the north, and was travelling with her friend Jean. I recalled afterwards that she said, 'I do hope we shall be friends!'

The time for boarding came and went and then the announcement that the plane had a mechanical fault and would not be able to leave that afternoon. We were taken all the way to Bournemouth, without our luggage which was already on the plane, and put up at a hotel there. The following morning, we were driven up to Heathrow again and, full of joyful anticipation, walked out through the boarding gate. I was just about to step through the door of the aircraft when the crew, doing their pre-flight checks, found a fault in the navigation equipment. Back we came to the lounge. There would be another wait while it was being repaired.

The airline staff were very apologetic. I felt no animosity towards them, but I was aware that the forces of darkness were intent on disrupting this tour and they were caught in the middle. It was time for direct action! We began to pray. We took authority over the evil powers that were working against us and entered into the victory which Jesus had won over them by His death and resurrection. We believed the promise in His word that 'We are more than conquerors through Him who loved us' and that 'No weapon formed against us would prosper'. The airline people are trained to maintain their poise in all kinds of situations but as the wave of prayer in English and in tongues rose up, from the kneeling group, they looked bemused. In a very short time the word came: the instruments were working. We could now board the plane! As we broke through the cloud over England into brilliant sunshine, my heart rejoiced and I remembered the Scripture:

> Thanks be unto God which always causeth us to triumph in Christ and maketh manifest the savour of His knowledge, by us, in every place.
>
> 2 Cor. 2:14

We visited the well-known sites around Israel and had the joy and privilege of seeing many of the places mentioned in Scripture. I was especially moved by the places which had not been built over and enshrined in large dark churches. Mount Carmel, where Elijah stood alone against the idolatrous prophets of Baal, the valley of Megiddo where the last great battle of Armageddon will take place, the quiet tomb in a garden just outside the modern walls of Jerusalem, which is believed to be the tomb in which the body of Jesus briefly rested, all brought a new consciousness of what 'Emmanuel, God is with us' meant to me. But on the last day, the great day of the Feast of Tabernacles, we left the tourist trail and returned to Jerusalem to march with six thousand other Christians from forty-five different nations, who had gathered to worship the Lord on that day, and to carry banners, which spelled out words of comfort to Israel. The visit was planned to give those who prayed for Israel an insight into the pressures on the nation and on Jews worldwide and we saw films and heard talks which added greatly to the value of the tour.

I had been to the Philippines, which is, in spite of Spanish and American influence, a purely Eastern country. Britain, in spite of having numbers of immigrants is a Western country. I found that Israel was different. It is a country where East and West meet and the tensions between them, which I knew from Scripture, are still as evident as ever. But whenever I had an opportunity, I ministered to Jew and Arab and Christian, to our coach driver, to Arab guides, to Israeli patients in hospital and to members of our party, and saw people saved, healed and delivered from demonic bondages. God blessed me and He enabled me to be a blessing.

On the plane coming back, there had been changes in the seat allocations and when I sat down, I found I had been placed next to Daphne and Jean. We talked for a little while, until I found myself dozing off and Daphne donned earphones and listened to music. Towards the end of the flight, the stewardess woke us up and we talked about where we were going when we landed. I said I would be picking up my Mini in London and heading for a week of meetings in Harlech. After that I hoped to go north to Merseyside to spend a few days with Dick and Mary. She told me that she lived further north and she mentioned Blackpool and somehow that stuck in my memory, although, as I subsequently found out, she lived way beyond there. When we were being told to fasten our seat belts for landing, she looked in her bag and found an address label and handed it to me. I took it, as she said what so many kind friends have said to me, 'If you're ever nearby, do come and see me and stay!' Well, I knew what a busy schedule I was returning to, and I thought it unlikely that I would ever have the opportunity to call, but I did not want to appear ungrateful, so I thanked her and put the address in my bag.

For four years now, I had lived out of a suitcase, moving constantly from place to place. I thought nothing of it, knowing that I was doing what God wanted. I had settled in my heart that I would trust Him in every circumstance and situation, even for the pillow on which I would lay my head. As I drove along unfamiliar roads, often late at night, in my little car, I did not feel frightened or lonely, it was on the contrary, an opportunity for fellowship with Jesus. I would sing praises, talk with Him and ask Him to give me understanding of His Word and to take care of the details of my life. Receiving answers in small things sometimes delighted me more than the big things.

At the end of my week in Wales I had a free weekend, followed by an invitation to speak at a dinner meeting at the Blackpool Chapter of Women's Aglow, on the Monday. The following Tuesday, Wednesday and Thursday I had tried to keep free to visit Dick and Mary at Bold, and I headed for there on that last Friday evening in October. I needed to sort out some winter clothes which were stored there, get my laundry done and repacked, telephone Ron, write some letters, review my programme, make sure that I was clear about the arrangements for meetings during November, as well as to have some quiet time to pray and meditate on the Word.

When I arrived, I found that they were not expecting me, but as always invited me to stay. On Saturday, while the washing machine was going Mary asked me about my programme. I told her about the Blackpool meeting but said, 'That's only an hour's drive up the M6 from here and I would like to come back immediately after the meeting'. 'Oh, Isabel, I am sorry,' Mary said, 'but I have just agreed that two missionaries on furlough should come on Tuesday, to stay till the weekend. I don't have any way of contacting them and we don't really have room to make everyone comfortable!' She was very concerned; 'Of course you can stay but it may be difficult for you to get all the things done you need to do'. I refused to be worried, because I believed that this was exactly the detail that God looked after. I then remembered the lady on the plane, who had given me her address and began to wonder if it was by God's leading that she had done so. I hunted around in my handbag but failed to find the label, so I dismissed the idea with the thought that if the Lord had wanted me to go there, I would not have lost her address. So I got on with the washing and ironing and spent the rest of Saturday putting things straight.

On Sunday, after lunch, we sat drinking coffee and Mary and Dick were quizzing me about the things that had been happening in my meetings and of course, about Israel. Mary was still concerned that I had nowhere quiet to spend the week and she brought up Daphne's name again. She was quite convinced that this encounter on the plane was significant and she pressed me to search my memory. I had to confess that all I was able to recollect was that her Christian name was Daphne and she lived at Blackpool. 'Well,' Dick said, 'If that's all we have and the Lord wants you to go there, then it must be enough. I will telephone the only contacts I have in Blackpool, the officers of the Full Gospel Businessmen's Fellowship, and see what we can find out!'. He went into the hall where the phone was and I called, 'Don't tell them it's me who wants to know, I feel so foolish about forgetting even her surname'. 'All right', Dick said, 'I won't mention your name'. I heard him dial the number and ask, 'Do you know someone called Daphne, who lives in Blackpool and who has just returned from a visit to Israel? A friend who met her would like to get in touch!' There was a pause; the man was consulting his wife. Dick heard the wife in the background say 'Is it Isabel Chapman who wants to know?'. So Dick, with his hand on the mouthpiece, said, 'They are asking if it's Isabel Chapman who wants to know! May I tell them?'. 'Oh yes!', I said in a resigned voice. God was in this somewhere and I was not being allowed to be anonymous. Dick was given a number to call in Blackpool and when I rang it and explained to the lady on the other end what I wanted, was told that Daphne did not live in Blackpool, but fifty miles away, and she was able to supply her telephone number. The ease and the speed with which this had been done staggered me. I never enquired how the various people deduced who Daphne was, it was enough that Mary had believed that God wanted me to go and He would get me there.

I telephoned Daphne and asked if I could take up her invitation to stay with her for a couple of nights. She was very happy to have me and went further by saying that she would come down to Blackpool for the meeting and accompany me back so that I would have no difficulty finding the way. The Lord was taking care of the details again. The ministry at Blackpool to those with needs went on until after midnight and Daphne sat watching and waiting till the end. I thanked the ladies of the Chapter, then we set off to find the Mini in the hotel car park. 'You must be tired', Daphne said, 'Would you like me to drive?' Without hesitation, I handed over the keys and got in on the passenger's side. It was the first time I had ever had a ride in that seat and I found it a pleasant change, especially when I realised what a competent driver Daphne was. As we chatted on the run up the M6, I learned that Daphne was a widow and a grandmother with seven grandchildren and was the same age as my mother. She had been a Christian for a long time and had a wide range of interests and knew a great many people all over the country. She did a lot of entertaining and loved having friends to stay. She was making me feel very welcome.

When we arrived I declined Daphne's offer of supper and she showed me to my room. I quickly got to bed and began to review the events of the day, to thank my Heavenly Father for all that He had done, for me and through me, that day, and for the bed He had provided. As I lay there quietly, thanking Him, I was aware of words coming into my consciousness from the Holy Spirit. 'This is the home that I have provided for you!'. I was absolutely astounded. My mind had not been dwelling on anything like that. It was true that, about six months earlier, the Lord had put a desire in my heart to have a home of my own again. At one time, it seemed possible that it was going to be in Norwich, more recently I had thought that it might be in the beautiful city of Bath. My own idea had been of somewhere compact, easily maintained and not too far from a motorway. But neither of these possibilities seemed to go beyond the point of my own thoughts and circumstances and I did not receive any prompting from God to go ahead. So I said sleepily, 'Lord, if that really was you who spoke to me, please give me confirmation; I will say nothing to Daphne'. Within minutes I was asleep.

I awoke the following morning and opened my curtains; the sun was shining. It would have taken a great artist and a large canvas to even begin to convey the sight and feeling of what I was looking at. A mixture of conifers and mature deciduous trees, in their autumn colours, framed a view down a valley. In the foreground, were smooth green lawns, merging into a shrubbery of every shade of brown and green, which flowed on into wild woodland. Through the trees I could catch glimpses of the blue waters of Morecambe Bay. Further away, the misty fells of the southern Lakes provided the backdrop to this wonderful combination of planned garden and nature.

We ate breakfast together. Daphne had some housework to see to but she refused my offer of help and sent me out to look at the garden. The morning sun had not yet dispersed the dew, which still sparkled around my shoes as I walked down between the high banks, clothed with such a diversity of growing things. I thanked God for His magnificent creation, and for its sheer abundance. As I descended further into that green glade, the house disappeared from sight, not a leaf stirred in the stillness, it was like finding a little piece of heaven on earth. I came back indoors, still submerged in the visual, emotional and spiritual wave which I felt had washed over me in the garden. Daphne was ironing and as I stood in the kitchen undoing my outdoor shoes, I tried to tell her about the impact the garden had made on me. The words came out in disjointed phrases. 'It's lovely Daphne, it's like heaven on earth, I've never known such a feeling of stillness. The Lord is so good, and He has been good to you'. Without pausing in her ironing, she said, 'If it's God's will, it's yours to share!' I stooped down to pull off my shoes, wondering how to respond to this extraordinary offer. I immediately recalled the Word I had received before going to sleep. Was this the confirmation I had asked for? It seemed to lack definiteness, so I pretended not to have heard, straightened up and went to find my indoor shoes. I was not sure that the words Daphne had just spoken came from her heart. So I just prayed 'Lord your will be done!' and waited. Over the next couple of days I found that the slight tension and guardedness which attach to first time visits, completely went; Daphne and I talked, laughed, prayed, read and worked together. The Lord was giving us His love and trust for each other.

'Would you like to take some flowers with you for Mrs Gregg? There are lots of chrysanths in the greenhouse'. I had just written down on a note pad the name and address where I would be staying in Derbyshire before setting off on the long drive south. Seeing the name of my next hostess had prompted Daphne's generous nature. I put my handbag in the Mini which was all packed, ready to go, and walked with her down to the greenhouse. While Daphne selected and cut the flowers, I stepped out of the greenhouse and walked a few steps to where a little stream ran through the glade, and tumbled over a tiny waterfall which made the water tinkle and sparkle in the autumn sun.

I found myself again experiencing the peace and beauty of the place but this time there was a new dimension to it. My heart was pounding, the warmth of the Holy Spirit enveloped me and I felt His love embrace me. It was as if God was letting me know that, what I had been experiencing over the last couple of days came out of His love for me. I was aware that His love was establishing a link between myself and this place, so that I would not just get into the car and drive away, as I did from so many other houses. As the experience deepened, I laughed, I cried, I felt as if my heart would explode. I had never experienced such love and it was almost more than I could bear. I had difficulty standing upright, I was staggering about, overwhelmed by the presence of the Lord. I cried out in tongues, unable otherwise to give expression to what I wanted to say to the Lord. At that moment, I desired nothing more than to stay forever wrapped up in His love. I was vaguely aware of Daphne coming out of the greenhouse, holding on to me to steady me and joining in, to pray with me. She knew that the Lord had touched me deeply. In between crying in the Spirit and laughing, I found myself apologising for my behaviour and trying to tell her that I did not normally carry on like this. A few minutes later, the tangible presence of the Lord left as suddenly as it had come. The effect however stayed with me all the rest of the day in a continuing special sense of God's love. We walked back to the car; I thanked Daphne for having me to stay and for the beautiful flowers, jumped into the car and watched her in the mirror waving cheerily to me as I drove off. All the way to Chinley, I was reacting normally to traffic and road conditions but I felt such a lightness in my spirit, that I wanted to tell every driver, every pedestrian I passed, that God loved them.

Before my first meeting, I went to the hall where I was to speak and joined Mr and Mrs Gregg and some of their friends, in a small side room, to pray for an hour. Facing me on the wall was a poster. I can't remember the text printed on it because my eyes went immediately to the group of conifers, lit by the rising sun, which it depicted. It was as though I was back in the garden, surrounded by the glory of God, and again, I felt myself so full of His love that I wept. I could not stop weeping tears of joy and the flood continued for much of that hour. I was embarrassed, wondering what the others were thinking. They were sensitive and continued to pray in tongues and in English. A few mintues before the meeting started, I regained some control over myself, and we started.

The Lord moved powerfully in that small community, particularly among those in their teens and twenties. I remember particularly, a meeting in a house, where a number of young people were sitting on the floor, and as I prayed that the Lord would baptise them in the Holy Spirit they toppled over where they sat as the power of God came on them. They were unusually open to hear what God wanted to do, in and through them. It was a joy to me to see them beginning to step out in faith and walk in power and demonstration of the Spirit. Many at the meetings came into a new knowledge of the word of God, which enabled them to receive their healing and glorify God in their bodies. There was, sadly, some opposition to what I said and did, from those whose view of the Bible was different to mine and those who were prepared to give a great deal of weight to religious traditions and humanistic ideas. But this did not stop God demonstrating His power and showing the people that He is a living God, who keeps His Word. I no longer felt the rebuffs in a personal way; God had taken me through that, but I was always concerned for those who had been prevented from realising that they were lost.

Daphne telephoned me at Chinley and when she found that I had a few days free before going to Poole pressed me to come and spend them with her. During those ten days while I had been at Chinley, Daphne had a growing conviction that it was God's will that she should share her home with me, though she hesitated about expressing it. For my part, I was becoming aware that the Lord was providing me not only with a home base but with a helper in the work that He had called me to do. I had been praying, asking the Lord that, if I had understood Him correctly, He would give me some direct confirmation. He gave me the reference 2 Corinthians 8:20, which I promptly looked up in my Living Bible and found 'If anyone asks you who Titus is, say that he is my partner, my helper in helping you!' So Daphne was to be my partner and helper and she was God's appointment; I was happy that the Lord had recruited such a competent, sympathetic and unflappable person to assist in the work. I decided, however, that I would again say nothing to her. I wanted her to know, personally from God, that it was His plan for her life at that time. So I again packed everything into the Mini. Daphne came out to the car to see me off and continued waving as I set off down the drive. At that moment, the rain started, and as I came to the end of the drive and could look out beyond the trees, there it was. A big bright rainbow arched across the top of the monkey-puzzle trees spanning the entrance gate. To me, since being born again, the rainbow had always been more than a pretty physical phenomenon. I knew from Scripture that it was the reminder of our covenant-making God. It was the last confirmation that I needed. I pushed the gear shift into reverse and sped backwards towards the house. Daphne had not moved from where I had left her. She had seen the rainbow and was standing with arms stretched upwards, praising the Lord. For her too, it had been the seal and confirmation of our partnership in the service of our Lord Jesus Christ. We stood there, not needing to speak, praising and worshipping the Lord together. Within five minutes, I was back in the car and on my way once again. When I reached the end of the drive the rainbow had gone. God's timing is perfect.

Chapter Nine

Daphne and I both believe that God has called us to work together. She says that the Lord told her to stay in my shadow to be a partner, helper and encourager. This she certainly has been, and as she reflected on her past experiences, it seemed that the Lord had been preparing her, over many years, for what He would have us do together, in His service. It is clear from the following testimony that she knew that God had something new for her to do, but she had no inkling of what it might be:

'My husband John, who was an army officer, died just five years before I met Isabel. We had been married thirteen years when he died; he was a charming, unselfish, much loved, true gentleman, with a great sense of humour, and a great love for his God, his fellow men and the countryside in which he lived. I was happy for him when he died, some people maybe thought strangely so, but I knew that he had gone to glory and that it would be but a twinkling of an eye before we would be together again. I just felt that the Lord wanted me to get on and do my best for Him during the life on earth left to me, and at this point I offered Him the whole of myself and all that I had.

'During that five years, I felt that the Lord was going to use me for something specific, but whenever I went to Him in prayer, thinking I'd got a good "idea" He always told me to "Tarry my pleasure" and so it was, that during this period of time, well supported by my prayer partner,

Jean, in particular, I learnt something about patience, and quite a lot about obedience.

'I was born again at my Confirmation in 1942, and I knew I wanted to know more of my Lord and Saviour. I know that sometimes I prayed for people and the Lord healed them, but I just felt a lack of power and I was aware that I needed knowledge as to how to pray in a particular situation. I felt too, that although I was learning all the time in countless experiences through which the Lord had taken me, I still had not reached that point at which I could say "that's the way He wants me to go".

'I joined in many social activities, as well as trying to stay aware of where the Holy Spirit wanted to guide me. I experienced as much as I could by listening to tapes, going to conferences, seminars and meetings. In 1982 I went to Israel to celebrate the Feast of Tabernacles. In 1983, I was baptised by the Holy Spirit, with the evidence of speaking in other tongues, and truly began to experience the power of the Holy Spirit that had been lacking all those years. It was in October 1984 that I paid my second visit to the Feast of Tabernacles. This was the year in which my life changed dramatically.

'At London Airport, I was moved to go over and speak to a lady, I don't know why, for I didn't know her, or who she was, or anything about her, I was just compelled to make enquiries. This was Isabel.

'In a most extraordinary way, the Lord drew me into a desire to pray in tongues on many occasions during that holiday, and though I hardly ever spoke to Isabel, I was made aware of her many times. I noticed how often she appeared to be fellowshipping with God, unaware of what was going on around her, or actually praying in tongues, presumably for the existing situation, wherever she happened to be, in the bus, in a shop or walking from one place to another.

'21 October 1984 was a red letter day for me. We were sightseeing that morning. I was standing on a high lay-by admiring the view of Israel below, when a rather breathless young Scottish lady, whom I didn't know before, because she was in the other half of our group, came racing up to me. She said, "I'm Kathy Scott, are you Daphne?". It turned out that, during prayers that morning, the Lord had given her a word for "Daphne" and she spent rather a long time finding out who Daphne was. Having been an Anglican all my life, I wasn't used to having "words from the Lord" so when she handed me a small scrap of paper, I was inclined to be super-attentive. On it was written these words – "You are a precious bud in his hand – As you are nurtured and watered in His love and power, you will blossom into a beautiful flower". My legs seemed to go to jelly as I read these words. "Why particularly" you may ask . . . Well . . . because I had decided, in obedience to the urging of the Holy Spirit, to be baptised in Lake Galilee that afternoon.

'I had not been home from Israel very long before I received another word from the Lord. "Cease to dwell on days gone by and to brood over past history, here and now I will do a new thing; this moment it will break from the bud. For I will pour down rain on a thirsty land, showers on the dry ground, I will pour out my Spirit on your offspring and every blessing on your children". Well, there was the confirmation for which I had been waiting, I just knew that my life was to completely change.

'You will have read elsewhere of how the Lord brought Isabel and I together; it was a divine appointment. I just knew that the Lord wanted us to work together. Somehow, all the skills that I had learnt in my earlier life became useful. The Lord had given me organisational skill, an ability to map read well, to enjoy driving, to love and care about people, to be adaptable, to enjoy telling people about what a wonderful God I have, and above all He gave me a knowledge that my whole life had been a training-ground for what He now wanted me to do. Offering Isabel a share in my home was easy, even giving up my golf, bridge and entertaining was easy. I was ready to give up the whole of my old way of life and just obey God's will for me, to be a partner, a helper and a supporter to Isabel and her calling.

'That part was easy; the opposition I experienced was less easy to bear. It came from both family and friends who simply did not understand . . . how could they? I just pray that they will all come into an understanding of the Gospel and that they, too, will receive their salvation. In that expectation, I stand on His word that He would pour out His Spirit on my offspring. I could hardly believe the blessing that surrounded me, helping Isabel at her meetings. I saw people saved, miracles, healings, people baptised in the Spirit and praying in tongues. Added to which, I was hearing the Word of God and slowly coming into the realisation of who I was in Christ Jesus, including that by His stripes I was healed nearly 2000 years ago, and my daily pill intake was slowly but surely reduced!'

Chapter Ten

'We hope that you will come back to the Philippines soon.'
That phrase kept recurring in letters from the pastors and
Bible School students I had met and continued to
correspond with. They gave me news about people and
places, of the political uncertainty and of their struggles to
set up new churches outside the towns and cities. They
were very constrained by lack of funds for travelling and
buying Bibles, Sunday school material and simple building
supplies.

When I accepted speaking engagements in Britain, I
never mentioned money or expenses, because I knew that if
I continued to submit my will to the will of my Father, He
would provide all my needs and also enable me to help
other members of His Body. So from time to time I would
check if my bank account had started to grow and would
clear out the surplus above my immediate needs and send it
to the Philippines. But they kept enquiring when I myself
was going back and I maintained an open heart before the
Lord on the question. During 1984, when I was already
receiving requests from all over Britain to speak at meetings
next year, the Lord made it clear to me that I should reserve
a four-month period at the beginning of 1985 for a second
visit to the Philippines.

The news that I was returning to the Philippines soon
spread and God began to reveal His purposes for the forthcoming mission. It was at that time that I met Philip and
Sheila White. They explained to me that they felt that God

was calling them to give up their jobs, sell their home and join me in the Philippines to film the work that the Lord was sending me there to do. As I saw that they were very earnest and willing to give up their worldly security for the sake of the Gospel, I was careful not to lead them in any way because it was important that they should know beyond any doubt that their call was from God. I knew that if it was truly God's will and they were open, He would work it out. We prayed together, confessing our desire to be in His perfect will. Afterwards, in my private prayer time I said 'Lord, if it is not your will that Phil and Sheila join me, please shut the door, don't allow them to come; now I leave the outcome in your hands'. Daphne too had begun to feel that she ought to accompany me to the Philippines and we had prayed together that God would reveal to us if that were His wish.

A month later, Philip and Sheila came to film a series of meetings at Portsmouth. They told me that they had put their house on the market and were working out their notice in their jobs. They would be ready to join me in the Philippines at the appropriate time, though I did not yet know which part of the visit the Lord was sending them to record. I let my contacts in the Philippines know that there was the possibility of filming some of the meetings, and asked them to draw up an outline programme with that in mind. We could then book the air tickets for the different departure dates, because I believed that I would go out first and begin a series of trips into the mountains. Being on the spot, I would try to fix a firm timetable for the continuation of the visit so that Phil and Sheila's time could be used effectively. The city visits could be left till the end and Daphne would join us for those, where her help would be most valuable. I was beginning to feel excited at the new things God was doing; this visit was not going to be just a repeat of the first. He had new adventures in store for us.

Chapter Eleven

Heathrow had been the gateway to the unknown when I had set out, five years earlier for the Orient, and what for me truly was the mysterious East. Where I should go, what I should do, whom I should meet, had all been hidden from me. Travelling by air was also a new experience and finding my way through the formalities had been a strain. Since then I had flown 60,000 miles and the bustle of Terminal Three on a mid-winter Monday morning was no longer a strange experience. Daphne had driven me down to London and now, as I waved a final goodbye before passing through Passport Control, I heard her call, 'See you in Manila'. The crowd closed round me and I moved with the crush into the departure lounge; I was on my own again.

The twenty-two hour flight offered an opportunity for quiet reflection. I slept little. I thought of the people I would be meeting in the next three months, many of whom had become close friends and who would be working with me to arrange itineraries, introduce me, act as guides and interpreters and be my companions on the way, as well as nurturing those converted during my visit. Like all long distance flights, time was punctuated by meals and in-flight films, but finally the lights were switched off and as the Middle East slipped past, thirty five thousand feet below in the moonlight, the passengers and cabin crew settled down. There was little noise apart from the background whine of the engines. I felt at peace. Then I was conscious of the Lord speaking to me, not in audible words but in structured thoughts which arose somewhere outside my own conscious processes. 'I am sending an angel before you to lead you safely to the land I have prepared for you. You must at all times walk in obedience to the prompting of my Spirit. You must be careful to obey and follow my instructions, and I will be an enemy to your enemies. You must not worship the gods of the people I am sending you to, nor sacrifice to them in any way and you must not follow the evil example of these people. You must utterly conquer them and break down their shameful idols. You shall serve the Lord your God only. Then I will bless you, provide for your every need and take sickness from among you. I will do marvels in thy midst and all the people in the nations round about you shall see the work of the Lord. Be very careful never to compromise with the people there in the land where you are going, for if you do, you will soon be following their evil ways. You must break down their heathen altars, smash their shameful idols; for you must worship no other god, but only Jehovah, for I desire absolute loyalty and exclusive devotion. The people in the land I am taking you to are spiritual prostitutes, committing adultery against me by sacrificing to their gods. If you become friendly with them, and one of them invites you to go with him and worship his idol, you must not. You must have nothing to do with idols'.

There was no mistaking that I was being given a very serious warning. I had met with idol worship at many different levels, both in primitive areas and among wealthy townspeople. I had not thought that I would ever be trapped into idol worship myself but I could see that a Christian might condone or ignore it, to avoid argument and hostility. It seemed that, in the war with Satan there was no room for a non-aggression pact. I digested these words for the rest of the flight.

When the plane door was flung open and I found myself

walking out on to the aircraft steps, the sudden change in temperature and humidity was an intensely felt sensation. Heat, reflected from the concrete runway and the white airport buildings, enveloped me in waves. The palm trees in the gardens, the brown faces, the tropical smells, the accents, informed all my senses that I was really back. However much my mind and spirit had been attuned to the idea, it was that moment which assured me that I really had arrived. Then I was being greeted by Susan, who had ministered with me in Laguna right at the end of my last stay. We had kept in touch by letter and when she had heard I was coming, had offered to meet me and put me up for the night. Her face lit up when she saw me, and she came forward, shyly and greeted me with a welcoming embrace. We found a taxi and set off for her parents' home in Manila, where she was now living. Soon we were in the thick of the desperately congested city traffic, which moved in fits and starts and all the time poured out exhaust fumes into the hot, humid air. As we sat in a succession of jams, perspiring, breathing in the sickening diesel fumes from buses and trucks which inhibited any conversation, I was in no doubt that the adventure had begun.

Like many houses away from the centre of the city, theirs was small, having just three rooms, a sitting room, bedroom and kitchen, under a corrugated iron roof; it accommodated seven people. When I climbed out of my London clothes and into the lightest dress I had, we went around the corner to enjoy an Americano hamburger at the local MacDonalds. As soon as we were seated, she began to tell me that when she heard that I was coming back to the Philippines, God had put it in her heart that she should arrange some meetings for me in Manila. She had in mind that these should not be in a church building but in the open air and had thought that somewhere she called Plaza Miranda would be suitable. The effect of the change in climate, and of the time zone difference, and of the Americano hamburger were beginning to tell on my concentration and I just nodded and made encouraging noises. For Susan it was an all-engrossing topic. Whenever I enquired about people I knew in Manila or the Bible Training Centre, or sister Mahan's activities, the conversation somehow kept shifting round to Plaza Miranda and those meetings. Susan continued to talk about them on the way back and while I undressed and installed myself in the one bed, which the family had given up for me. Finally she asked, 'Isabel, could you come with me tomorrow to see if you think the Plaza is suitable?' 'That is not possible,' I explained, 'I have to catch an early bus to San Fernando in the morning, they are expecting me there and will have made arrangements.' So we prayed together and I asked the Lord to lead her so that all aspects of these meetings would be in accordance with His will. 'There's something else', she said, 'We will need a permit from the mayor's office to hold the meeting and they may not take me seriously, so I was hoping that you would come there with me too.' Again we lifted the whole situation before the Lord and asked Him to overrule in every detail so that permits would be obtained.

Susan switched off the light and sleepy voices wished us good night from the various parts of the house where the rest of the family had settled down for the night. I lay back, conscious of the oppressive heat, but by now so exhausted that nothing, or so I thought, could keep me awake. As the house became quiet, except for the regular breathing of all its sleeping occupants, I was aware of a new sound. From somewhere close to the bed there was a continuous scratching sound. I whispered, 'What's that noise, Susan?' 'It's nothing, only rats,' came the sleepy reply. I pulled the sheet over my head. The scratching noises grew louder. Now, I could hear squeaks, which I guessed came from a nest of baby rats, and then sounds of movement on the concrete floor as they searched for food. I knew they would find it, because I had earlier seen a large bowl full of a dry cake mix which Susan's mother had prepared to take to market the following morning. Plop! a soft weight dropped from the rafters on to the bed and ran across my legs. I sprang upright and pressed against the wall, not daring to step off the bed. Susan's voice came from the darkness. 'Don't worry, Isabel, they will not harm you'. 'Are you sure they won't bite?', I asked anxiously. Susan obviously felt that a soothing reply was called for. 'It's really OK, Isabel, if they bite you I will kill them', she said. The cultural gap was yawning wide, too wide for me to cope with at that time of night, but I was not going to take any chances on being disturbed. So I prayed to my Father in heaven and asked Him to keep us safe from the rats and as an extra safeguard I spoke to those rats and commanded, in the name of Jesus, that they stay away from my bed. Then I lay down and just rested in the Lord, focusing my thoughts on Jesus and His care for me, and was soon sound asleep.

Early next morning, the sound of traffic from the nearby main street penetrated the unglazed window and dragged me into reluctant wakefulness. I got up, washed and dressed, and even though it was still not long after sunrise, my clothes were clinging to my body from the slight exertion of getting dressed. Susan's mother made me an omelette for breakfast, a generous act of hospitality, in a land where the cost of fresh eggs is out of reach of most people; it was the only one I was to eat in my whole stay.

On the way to the bus station, Susan's mind was again on the meetings she was going to arrange for me on my return to Manila. I gave her the only two dates that were absolutely firm, Daphne's arrival in Manila, when I planned to be there to meet her, and our flight back to England six weeks later. The meetings could be fitted in any time during that period but it would save unnecessary travelling if they could be at the beginning or end of that period. Susan decided to aim for the earlier date and I was happy with that. We said our farewells and I found a seat on the bus bound for San Fernando, 170 miles away to the north west. It was a relief to leave the teeming streets of the capital behind and enter the less hurried world of traditional country crafts and fieldwork. The area immediately north of the city is one of the few low-lying areas of Luzon; but the mountains were never far away and as we travelled north, over to my left I could just make out the mountains of Zambales, with their shapely volcanic cones surrounded by little wisps of cloud.

I was looking at the people and places with eyes not yet accustomed to my surroundings and the contrasts with home still stood out; the Malay and Chinese facial features, the reminders of Spanish influence especially in church buildings. In the towns, the general untidiness of the street scene and the modern buildings, which were of the plainest and most utilitarian kind and in need of paint testified to a society with no money to spend on frills. And everywhere there were children, beautiful, round faced brown-eyed smiling children. Toddlers playing on the roadside, in the charge of sisters little older than themselves contrasted with their elders, who were on the way to school wearing smart school uniforms.

Three hours later I caught my breath as the Cordilleras came into view; these were the spectacular mountains to which the Lord had brought me five years before and given me a ministry there. But now the bus was turning round their western flank and starting the final stage of the journey along the narrow strip of fertile land between the mountain range and the South China Sea. Glimpses of blue sea and white beaches alternated with misty peaks as the bus weaved its way along the undulating, winding road. It looked deceptively cool, but I knew the labourers, in their wide brimmed straw hats, working in the sugar plantations and tobacco fields would soon be forced into the shade for their midday siesta. I had learned from previous experience to take an air-conditioned coach, which at only a small extra cost would allow me to arrive in much better shape. I reflected what a key element transport was in the work I had come to do. The three main north-south routes were well served by buses between large towns, but once off these routes the roads into the much more sparsely inhabited interior were often no better than dirt tracks. The people who lived in these areas had to be self-contained, living off what the land provided or could be made locally. Their access to a town was by jeepney, a vehicle like a large Land Rover with seats for ten but normally carrying twice that number. These ran a once-a-day service to a string of villages along a dirt road and took the villagers who could afford the fare to town, to trade rice and beans and handicrafts for tinned food and other products of civilisation. Of course, there were many small villages at the end of long rugged trails away from any road, which could only be reached on horseback or on foot; but there were no horses! For me, the once-a-day service meant that each leg of a relatively short journey could take a day, so that a trip which ought to be covered in four or five hours could easily take three days, if I were to rely on public transport.

San Fernando was the town to which that record sleeve had brought me five years before, and now as I found my way to Miracle Mission where I had been lovingly received, I relived those moments. The site, on a hill overlooking the sea, was as beautiful and peaceful as I remembered it. The Rev. Clive Shields who had founded the mission had gone home to glory soon after my return to England and his son Loren had come from America with his wife Darella and their young children, to continue the work. They had been joined by Stuart and Betty Dahl, who, having finished one career, had left family and friends in the USA, in obedience to God's call. They had a spare room and invited me to stay with them; they also had with them Lisa, a girl in her teens spending a school holiday with them. These were all new faces, who were to become friends, in the days ahead, but among the other staff were those who had received me as a total stranger and some had travelled with me, smoothing the way, introducing me, translating for me, sharing in worship and ministry and had corresponded with me in the intervening years; they were like family and we greeted one another as brother and sister.

The jeepney which I had purchased for them was still going well and was an indispensable part of their equipment, so much so, that it was with some diffidence that I asked if I could borrow it. Loren kindly agreed to drive us on the long trip to Tabuk and we fixed the date. I had already formed an outline plan of the time I would spend in different areas based on the contacts with the pastors who had helped me before and though I would be spending a much shorter time in the Philippines I hoped that, by making prior arrangements and having more reliable transport, I could go more deeply into remote areas than the Lord had taken me before. In the first stage, I had arranged to visit Pastor Eduardo Padua who lived just outside Baguio, a city at the end of the great Cordillera mountain range, and only thirty five miles from San Fernando. From that base we would visit mountain villages accessible from there. Then in stage two, I would go further north, well away from cities, to revisit Pastor Teckney at Tabuk, a base from which to visit some very remote and unevangelised villages. For stages three and four, I would return south to Manila and Dagupan.

I went over these plans with Loren and we thought that, balancing the needs of the mission against the transport difficulty of the various stages, it would be most useful to me to have the use of the jeepney in stage two. I was grateful for that, but I was not aware, at that moment of the additional transport burden into which the Lord was about to lead me! Pastor Abe, an old friend at the mission, mentioned that it would be a great asset in the remote villages if we had some good lighting. Paraffin pressure lamps were all very well to light up a Bible, but they left the congregation in darkness. In places where there had never been electric lighting, it would be a great draw to the villagers to gather to see the bright lights. I remembered that Phil White had mentioned that he would only be able to film after dark if electricity were available, and had suggested that I buy a generator, but it was the kind of technical detail that did not impress itself on me. But now, when Pastor Abe spoke, it impressed itself very strongly indeed, so forcefully, in fact, that I recognised God telling me that I should buy a generator, a public address amplifier, two microphones, ten of the longest fluorescent tubes I could find and yards of cable and rope. I consulted Pastor Abe about where I could buy all this and he said that, for the large items, we would have to look outside San Fernando and suggested Dagupan, forty miles away. He offered to drive me, and we set off and did indeed find shops where they were all in stock. I listed all the prices we were quoted and was amazed at what the total came to. If I bought it, I would only be left with a few hundred dollars out of the thousand I had brought with me to cover the cost of the entire visit.

All sorts of reasons filled my mind as to why I should not buy the equipment. There were practical reasons like, I had managed without it before, so it was not absolutely necessary; it would be hard to transport and someone who knew how to work it and connect it up would have to be at hand. Even more convincing were prudent reasons like, how would I possibly survive without any money in a poverty-stricken land; I could even be stranded in some remote hostile area, with no money for transport back to Manila for the flight home. So, having reasoned out the situation with my natural mind, I took the sensible decision not to buy it. Immediately, the Holy Spirit spoke to my spirit and said, 'Have I not told you that, at all times you must walk in obedience to the prompting of my Spirit and to be careful to obey all my directions. I desire you to purchase this equipment, for I shall use it for my glory'. Instantly and deliberately, I banished from my mind all my own reasoning and chose to walk in obedience, submitting my will to the will of my Father.

All this had happened more quickly than it takes to tell. Pastor Abe had been watching my face, no doubt wondering what this inscrutable Westerner was thinking. 'Right', I said, 'let's find a bank where I can cash my travellers cheques!' As we returned to the shops with a large bundle of hundred pesos notes, and I contemplated the few remaining travellers cheques, too slender a resource by far, for the journeys I and the teams were about to embark on, I did not dare reason how I would manage. But the Lord knows what is in our hearts and again the Holy Spirit spoke to my spirit, 'My grace is sufficient for you'. We brought the equipment back to Miracle Mission, where it would be looked after until we set out for the mountains.

Chapter Twelve

'Can I come with you Isabel?' Lisa asked. She had heard me telling Stuart and Betty about my previous visit and my plans for the next few weeks. I hesitated, wondering if she understood how different living conditions would be compared to rural America. I knew that the next few weeks were likely to be uncomfortable rather than physically dangerous; that would come later. I looked at Betty and Stuart who nodded and it was agreed. Next morning Pastor Abe drove us to Cruz La Trinidad, a small town on the edge of Baguio, where Eduardo Padua pastored a church. He was now the presiding pastor of his denomination, having succeded Pastor Teckney, who held that office when I had been here before. When he wrote to tell me that Pastor Teckney had retired, he had suggested that I should work with him, and said that he would assemble a team and make some preliminary arrangements.

In the Philippines I had never selected the people with whom I would work; the Lord had brought me and them together in situations which were not of my arranging. And now as another of these encounters was about to take place, I wondered what these new pastors, with whom I was going to share the rigours and toils of the next five weeks, would be like. Abe was married to Pastor Padua's wife's sister, so he knew him well. As we drove, he was able to tell me about his activities especially his enthusiasm for evangelism and starting new churches in the villages. As the jeepney climbed upwards towards the coolness of the mountain city,

I prayed 'Lord this is your appointment. I thank you for the people I am going to meet and work with and believe that you will fill our hearts with your love so that it will overflow to each other'.

We stopped outside a neat little two-storey wooden house. 'This is Padua's house', Abe said, 'he lives on the ground floor. Come and meet him.' He was a younger man than I had expected from his seniority in the church, but with a seriousness and dignity that I had found to be typical of the pastors I had met in the Philippines. He introduced me to his wife Marilyn and his sister-in-law Elizabeth who lived with them. The home had two tiny bedrooms, one of which was given to Lisa and I. The jeepney was required back at the mission as soon as possible but Filipino hospitality would not allow brother-in-law Abe to return without refreshment. So we sat down together and were soon getting to know one another, as the mixture of English and Ilocano conversation flowed. Sometimes, they forgot that I did not understand Ilocano (or any of the other 86 Filipino languages for that matter) and would look to me for comment. Then we would all laugh and Padua or Abe would quickly translate, so that I could rejoin the conversation. Communications in the Philippines were always a mystery. There were very few telephones and the service, using forty-year-old, mostly manual exchanges, was very unreliable and was in any case confined to the larger towns. But somehow messages seemed to get passed along, for when we arrived at Santo Thomas, we were expected.

Getting ourselves there had been quite an undertaking. First we had to find a jeepney driver who would be prepared to undertake the one hour drive into the nearby mountains, over some very rough roads and wait for us. This proved impossible, but Pastor Padua did find one prepared to take us there, and that from very close at hand. A young couple, whose first baby had just been born, occupied the upper part of the Padua's house and the husband, Jacob, operated a jeepney locally under an arrangement with a taxi proprietor in Baguio. Jacob was prepared to take us as close to Santo Thomas as the jeepney could manage but, because of the new baby, he wanted to come straight back. He drove us along a dirt road to the rim of a valley and pulled up opposite a gap in the trees lining the roadside. He pointed to the steep track that wound its way down through the rocks and in his broken English said, 'Santo Thomas there', and pointed down. It was walking time!

There were a few Christians in the village, among them an old lady in whose house the meeting was to be held. When we arrived she was preparing a meal for us, and we sat on the floor and ate it, as the word was spread through the village, that the pastor and a white lady had come. The dish she had prepared was mainly rice but contained diced pieces of ham and a green root vegetable that tasted like asparagus. By the time we had finished eating, practically the whole village, men, women and children, had gathered and were crammed together on the floor of the living room and overflowing into the sleeping quarters. In a village house there is usually neither furniture nor doors to limit the space, so they all could see and hear as Pastor Padua translated.

I spoke about God's love for them and about Jesus who had died to save them and about the Holy Spirit with which the Disciples were filled on the day of Pentecost. Almost everybody responded to the call for salvation and received Jesus as their Lord and Saviour and at least six people received their new heavenly language. The Lord had led me to pray for the sick and in this first meeting of my second visit to the Philippines He 'confirmed His word with signs following'. The first man had a lot of pain in his abdomen and Pastor Padua told me that he had said he had a stomach ulcer. When I prayed, the Lord instantly healed him. His joy raised the faith of the rest and they began to come forward. I remember we prayed for a girl with a bad cough, who said that she felt a cool breath of air passing through her lungs. We found later that she was suffering from tuberculosis and had been completely healed. Three of the men who had repented and believed were addicted to alcohol and tobacco and asked me to pray that they would be set free. After I prayed, I suggested that they burn their stocks of tobacco. It was evidence of the way the Holy Spirit had convicted and delivered them, that they complied.

The hike back up the rocky path was a hazardous undertaking in the dark. We linked hands and followed in single file. The man in front, who had a torch, called out the position of potholes and boulders on the track. We all made it safely to the road. But here we were an hour's drive from Cruz La Trinidad and the chance of a lift seemed remote. I gathered the team around me and we prayed 'Lord, please send us some transport'. Then we started to walk. We had been walking for about an hour without sight of even a bullock cart, when the lights of a car appeared. We stood in the middle of the road and waved it down. It was an empty truck. What it had been doing on this remote road so late at night we never found out, but we saw it as the Lord's answer, and piled in. The driver was very taciturn and even glowing accounts of the miracles of healing we had just witnessed did not move him, but he saved us many hours of walking.

We repeated the visit to Santo Thomas the following day, but this time Jacob agreed to return for us. When I prayed about the theme on which I should speak, the Lord led me to the sixth chapter of Ephesians, and when I spoke to my interpreter for the evening he said the Lord had prompted him to read that chapter in preparation. This was an encouraging confirmation and gave me an additional boldness in assuring these new Christians that, not only were their sins forgiven through Jesus, but He would enable them to resist the devil and to overcome sin in their lives. The message went home and many afterwards came, confessing areas of sin in their life and fell under the power of God, when we prayed for their deliverance. I asked some of those who had been healed the night before to stand up and tell about it. When they had finished a mother brought her daughter to me and said she had cancer in one arm, she was in continuous pain and was unable to move her arm. We rebuked the evil spirit in the name of Jesus and commanded that it leave her. Then we prayed in tongues; for this situation I felt we needed to yield our voices to the Holy Spirit who would bring into being the healing that God had provided in the body of Jesus. 'By whose stripes ye were healed.' (1 Pet. 2:24.) Within minutes she was lifting her arm up over her head, moving it round easily and all pain had gone. The joy and relief that showed on the mother's face touched me and brought a fresh revelation to me of God's love for His people and His wish to meet their needs.

When Jacob heard that we wanted to go to Longlong he threw up his hands. The roads in that area were very steep he said, and the surface had been washed away and the jeepney was likely to be damaged. He was however, persuaded to try and we soon found ourselves traversing the worst excuse for a road I had ever experienced. Poor Jacob; the dirt road was one continuous series of potholes, frequently with a deeper cavity into which the wheels descended with a sickening thud, often wrenching the steering wheel out of his control. He was concerned for the tyres and springs, while we were more aware of the effect on our anatomy. The seats were steel benches with practically no upholstery and every break in the road surface produced a bone shaking shock as we clung to the frame to keep ourselves from being flung about. Sometimes a wide trench, the full width of the road, would appear and since, for most of the way, we were spiralling up a mountain, with a cliff on one side and a steep drop on the other, there was no way round. The solution was to get out, gather stones and fill in the trench sufficiently to pass. This happened so frequently that we made better progress by having one of the team walk ahead to spot and fill in the impassable holes. A few times the holes were so deep that he had to call for help to manhandle large boulders to fill them. All this took place to the mutterings of Jacob about what was happening to the jeepney, but God be praised, we arrived without accident even if we were bruised and shaken. As the village came into sight I was so relieved that we did not have to finish the journey on foot that I shouted 'Praise the Lord' loudly and scrambled down.

I was aware that a pleasant smell which I had been noticing for the last few minutes was coming from the village, and it was so unexpected that it took some time to identify it. It was strawberry jam! Up here, the climate was cooler and wetter, which just suited strawberries and the villagers grew them and made them into jam in large iron pots, over open fires. The jam was carried by the occasional jeepney which came that way and sold in the market in Baguio. As I walked around the village, I gradually acquired a tail of children, who slowly overcame their shyness at the sight of this strange visitor with the brown hair and white skin. They were dressed in rags, but some had no clothes at all, and were running barefoot over the rocky ground. Their hair was matted and dirty and infested with lice, causing them to scratch continuously. I produced some sweets and soon all barriers were down, they chattered excitedly and the bolder ones took my hand. In villages where churches had been established, I had seen children singing in English and doing the actions to choruses. I wondered whether that would be possible here. Alex fetched his guitar and sat down on a rock as we gathered the children into a group around him. Then with Alex playing and singing and Lisa and I joining in with actions, we found that they soon picked up the words even though they had no idea what they meant. Later perhaps a church would be established and they would hear. By now the village was settling down to its evening routine, and in every house the rice pot was boiling ready for the return of the men. Again accompanied by the children, we visited each of the little wooden houses with their thatched roofs and, with the help of the interpreter, invited the parents to come to a meeting that evening.

On the way back to the home of our hostess, who had been preparing a meal for us, there was a loud honking noise and the children rapidly let go my hand and fled. I was left standing wondering what was happening. From between the houses a hissing fury of feathers emerged, neck outstretched and wings flapping. I followed the children's example and ran. The sight of the overdressed, white lady tearing round the village with a yellow beak hissing and snapping at her heels, was too much for the onlookers. They grinned, they chuckled, they doubled up in gales of laughter, everyone, men, women and children rushed to their doorways to see me pant past. I did not think it at all funny being chased by a bad tampered gander and when it appeared that he was not going to stop until he had driven me out of the village, I decided it was time to show I had dominion over him! I gripped my headscarf, turned round, swiped his head with it and yelled, 'In Jesus' name you stay away from me'. He stopped, backed away and let me know in no uncertain terms that he did not like me and resented my being in his village. The hissing changed to honking and he continued to follow me and honk, now at a respectful distance, for a full twenty minutes. I had so obviously hurt his feelings by flicking my scarf that I felt I had to apologise, in the hope of stopping the row. So I said contritely, 'I am very sorry for offending you, Mr Gander, but you really have made enough fuss about it now'. The apology was not accepted and as I went indoors to sit down to the meal I could hear him protesting, to all who would listen that there was a stranger in the village! 'What a way to break the ice', I thought, 'now they all know I'm here.'

From where I sat crosslegged, on the floor, I could see suspended above the doorway the skeleton of a snake, and I remarked that it was a strange form of decoration. Pastor Padua said, 'I don't think it is for decoration', and turned to our host, who with much gesturing explained, and it was translated for me, that it was believed snakes could not drown, so when on a journey that involved fording a river, he would wear the snake skeleton on his head, so that the spirit of the snake would keep him safe. I had heard that the Igorot people higher up the mountain were animists and sacrificed to demons. Up there, when one of the family got sick, the father went to consult the tribal faith healer, bringing a chicken or a pig to be sacrificed in a ritual way. After the sacrifice, I was told, the sick person was sometimes healed, but the healing usually lasted only a short time because the spirits wanted another sacrifice. Successive sacrifices frequently drove families into debt when their own meagre livestock was used up. Longlong was not an Igorot village and must have been in occasional touch with Christianity for centuries but here too, it became clear, the people were terrified of the spirit world and often resorted to faith healers.

After our meal, I went outside to find a quiet place, away from the children and the noisy gander, to be alone with the Lord. As I prayed, the word of the Lord came to me, 'You must not worship the gods of these people, nor sacrifice to them in any way. You must not follow the evil example of these people, you must utterly conquer them and break

down their shameful idols, and smash their heathen altars.'
I prayed in my heavenly language for some time and
believed that God was giving me knowledge and understanding of how to smash down their heathen altars and
idols. I opened my Bible and read:

> Thou shalt have no other gods before me. Thou shalt
> not make unto thee any graven image, or any likeness of
> anything that is in heaven above or that is in the earth
> beneath, or that is in the water under the earth: Thou
> shalt not bow down thyself to them, nor serve them: for
> I the Lord thy God am a jealous God, visiting the
> iniquity of the fathers upon the children unto the third
> and fourth generation of them that hate me; and
> shewing mercy unto thousands of them that love me,
> and keep my commandments.
>
> Exodus 20:3–6

This was the text upon which I was to base my sermon.
How I was to present it to these people, whose ideas and
attitudes to things of the spirit were evidently very different
to mine, I did not know. I knew the Holy Spirit would give
me words to bridge the gap. I got the team together and as
the people gathered in the house, I told them what the Lord
had given me to speak on and we prayed together in the
Spirit until it was time to start.

As soon as I got up to speak I was conscious of the
anointing of the Holy Spirit and words poured out of my
mouth. Often, when that had happened before, I had not
been able to remember afterwards much of what I had
spoken, but this time words impressed themselves on me, as
though the Lord would be requiring me to speak them
again. The words came so freely and powerfully that I had
to check from time to time to allow the interpreter to catch
up. I remember saying, 'God has forbidden us in his Word

to make for ourselves graven images of any kind. We are not to bow down to them nor serve them, for the Lord God is a jealous God. Why pray to a dumb idol that can neither see nor hear nor talk? The living Lord Jesus Christ who knows and sees all things is waiting to hear your prayers. He sits at the right hand of God the Father forever making intercession for us. He is the one who brings the light every morning, and the darkness every night. He is the one who sends the rain in the rainy season to water the ground, so that crops can grow. God says, if you love me, you will keep my commandments, you will smash your gods which really are no gods at all. How stupid and shameful it is to believe that a dumb idol can hear or answer your prayers. Turn from these heathen pagan ways, repent of your sins and God will forgive you, for he loves you. But He is a jealous God and demands absolute loyalty and exclusive devotion. Jesus shed His sinless, spotless blood once, for all. Jesus allowed His body to be beaten and lashed so that we could be healed. Sickness, pain, disease, depression, oppression and mental disorder are all the works of the devil. Jesus bore our sickness and carried our pains so that we do not have to. You must stop making sacrifices to the devil. If you turn from these heathen pagan ways, Jesus will fill you with the Holy Spirit. The Spirit of God dwelling within you will give you power over all the works of the devil. Instead of making sacrifices to the devil and trying to appease him, you will speak to the evil spirit and command it to leave, for all that is of darkness must obey the name of Jesus. The name of Jesus is more powerful than anything in heaven, or on the earth or under the earth. If you are willing to turn your backs on these devilish practices and make Jesus Christ Lord of your life, and worship no other god, will you please raise your hand, so that I can lead you in a prayer of repentance?'

At that point a few people left the meeting, they refused

to respond to the word of God. All who remained raised their hands. I led them in a prayer of repentance, and they renounced their pagan practices. Jesus filled them with the Holy Spirit and most of them spoke with other tongues as the Spirit gave them utterance. The Lord showed the people that He is a living God, by confirming His word with signs following. As well as salvation and the miracle of speaking in tongues, the ears of the deaf were opened and a young man was delivered of alcohol addiction, smoking and stealing. As they responded to the word of God, the blessings of the everlasting covenant automatically came upon them.

It was close to eleven o'clock when we finished and we set out to renegotiate the potholes back to Baguio, a process made all the more hazardous by the inky blackness. Jacob soon faced another difficulty; there were no road signs of any kind and no visible landmarks outside the patch of light from the headlamps. It was sometimes impossible to tell when we came to a fork, which was the main track. Three times we made the wrong choice and drove for miles over even worse roads, which wandered around in circles, bringing us back to a junction we had passed earlier. We were getting more and more bruised by the pounding and I was concerned that we might run out of petrol. At one point we headed down a track which came to a dead end with no room to turn around and Jacob could only reverse back the way we had come. On a steep section, he got the back wheels on to a patch of wet sand and we came to a halt with the engine screaming and sand being flung in all directions. He tried going forward and then charging back at the soft patch but always came to a halt in the same place. 'Lord', I prayed, 'you promised that your angels would be with me. Please tell them to give us a push.' Pastor Mark decided to give the angels a hand and got out to push; this time the jeep roared through the sand.

The aimless wandering of the jeepney and the continual pounding to which we were subjected by the state of the roads, coming at the end of a long day had reduced the team to a despondent silence, and for Lisa it must have been quite frightening. I started to talk about the things we had seen that day, but it was not the miracles which lifted their spirits but their recollection of my flight from the goose. 'No wonder you are tired, Isabel', someone said, and off they went into guffaws again. So we got to Cruz La Trinidad in good heart, even though it was in the small hours.

It happened that we had not planned a trip out on the following day, so we had the luxury of a late start, after which Lisa and I caught a bus into the centre of Baguio. The time had come to cash the last of the traveller's cheques so that we could pay for the jeep hire for the following week. As soon as I got the cash, I went to the telephone exchange to ring Daphne. This was my first attempt to communicate with her since my arrival, and I knew from past experience that it would entail a lot of waiting even if the system was working well. However, I did get through and was able to ask her to get in touch with Ron Taylor to find if there was any money left in the ministry account and to ask him to send it out with Phil and Sheila White. I told her about the desperate need for transport, both for the completion of what I had come to the Philippines to do and for the ongoing work among the villages by the local pastors.

When I had come to the point, back in Dagupan, of following the Lord's instructions about spending most of 'my' money on electrical equipment my own previous thoughts on how the trip was to be financed flew out of the window. The Lord had provided that thousand dollars and I had seen it as being sufficient to pay for the transport and the daily expenses of the team, but it now seemed that, all along, He had a different use for that money. When I had left England I had emptied my bank account, so I had no reason to expect that Ron could immediately send me a substantial amount to replace what I had spent. But I was not concerned because somehow God had it in hand and I got on with the work into which He led me each day. I did not know until much later what started to happen ten thousand miles away after I had phoned Daphne as the Lord worked out His purposes and answered our prayers.

As Daphne reflected on what I had said on the phone, she found herself getting anxious that the work in the Philippines was being hindered by lack of suitable transport. She knelt and asked the Lord to make it possible for her to bring enough money with her to buy a jeepney, when she came to join me. The Lord answered her prayer by giving her many unexpected opportunities to tell a wide audience of our urgent need for a vehicle. A newspaper reporter turned up seeking information for an article about what I was doing in the Philippines and he emphasised our transport difficulties in his article, which was reprinted by many local newspapers in the North-West. The local BBC radio station interviewed Daphne and again the message went out. Wherever and to whoever Daphne spoke she mentioned the jeepney; it had really become 'a desire of her heart'. Shortly after, on a Sunday evening, she was driving up the M6, returning home from visiting a relative. As she approached Lancaster, she found herself thinking about St Thomas' church and realised that if she turned off the motorway, she could be there in time for Evening Prayer. It took her a little longer than she expected and the service was already underway, so she slipped quietly into a back pew. Daphne knew that this was a church in which there was opportunity for people to move in the gifts of the Spirit, so was not surprised when a woman stood up during a pause in the service and began to prophesy: 'The Lord has given me a word of prophecy for someone in the congregation', she said in a quiet voice and went on in a firmer tone, 'I will not send you empty-handed and I will reveal my purposes to you when you are on the mountain'. As she spoke the words, Daphne experienced the power of God around her. It felt as if her chest was being crushed by a powerful blow which did not hurt but suspended her breathing. The words she had just heard filled her mind and so impressed themselves on her that she knew they were for her. God had spoken to her. The frustration she had felt on my behalf vanished and was replaced by a spirit of praise.

With every day that passed, God was touching the hearts of His people and through the letterbox came a stream of letters with cash and cheques for large and small amounts which built up a total sufficient to buy a good jeepney. Over in Norwich, Ron too was finding money flowing in; I had emptied the ministry account, now this too was being replenished. The Lord was ensuring that there would be something for Phil and Sheila to bring out to me to pay our expenses.

Chapter Thirteen

'Since you were here in 1981, Isabel', Pastor Padua said, 'the New People's Army has become a much bigger menace'. I had been discussing with him the second phase of my visit from a base at Tabuk and he had been at pains to stress the dangers inherent in excursions outside the towns. 'Discontent with the government of President Marcos is very widespread', he continued. 'Arms are being obtained from Communist sources. The NPA also seem to be arming the tribespeople, who have very little idea about politics but are delighted to be given a high power rifle. The NPA obtain food and supplies by raiding villages or ambushing vehicles. As well as disliking the Marcos government, they hate Western capitalists and Christian preachers. So you would be a target on both counts. It would be an extremely risky thing for you to do, to visit the places you went to on your last visit, and if you pressed on further you would be going to places which the army and police rarely, if ever, visit. There is also a practical point; the tribal language is spoken over a relatively small area. None of us could interpret for you and it really needs a Christian from the area. It would almost certainly be necessary too, to be brought there by someone known to the village who would vouch for you.'

I understood Pastor Padua's concern for me and the responsibility he felt for my welfare. He also had to think of his own and the team's safety, so it was important that I fully understood the dangers and did not embark on the trip lightly. I knew from the experience of my first visit that the NPA danger was an addition to an already hazardous situation. The tribal people high up in the mountains engaged in intertribal warfare and were very suspicious of strangers. They were also head-hunters; their initiation rituals and admission to the eldership of the tribe required that they bring back a human head. Although more extensive policing was reducing this activity in accessible areas, I remembered that five years earlier when I was in Tabuk a headless body had been found on the edge of the town.

We needed to be in agreement on where the Lord wanted us to go and to let Pastor Teckney know our schedule, so we all gathered to pray. It was quite a large group; Pastor Padua, Elizabeth and Lisa and I were joined by Alex the 'song leader' and Pastor Mark who would assist with the interpreting. We prayed in English, but also in the Spirit, seeking to know the will of God. I had found that the statement of Paul in Romans 8:26 was indeed a way forward when one did not know 'What we should pray for, as we ought', but to allow 'the Spirit to make intercession for us with groanings that cannot be uttered'. So we yielded our voices to the Holy Spirit, praying in other tongues. God prayed into being His will and revealed to us the way we should take. We became of one mind that we should go high up into the mountains of the province of Kalingo Apayao, and visit villages around Tabuk some of which had not previously heard the Gospel. We then got down to the actual schedule. I knew I would like to revisit the villages I had ministered in before but also to go beyond Lewan into completely unevangelised areas. Pastor Padua said that we should make a timetable up to Lewan and then allow a few more days to go beyond there, but it would depend on finding a local guide and Christian interpreter. He promptly wrote to Pastor Teckney giving him this information.

There was one more trip planned from Cruz La Trinidad, to which I was looking forward, even though it required a four and a half hours journey! Palatong, which was near the gold mines at Palasaan, remained in my memory for many reasons, not least because it was the place I had first preached to a village congregation in the Philippines. Jacob, who was becoming much more friendly and was clearly touched by the things he had been seeing and hearing, agreed to drive us. I paid him in advance and realised I had only a few hundred pesos left (about £20).

As we were driving along, it occurred to me that the following day would be Sunday and back home in Norwich they would be having a communion service. I wondered what happened at Palatong and I was told it was unlikely that they would be having a communion, indeed my companions guessed they might never have had a communion service there. I afterwards found that this was, in fact, the case. As we jolted along a road, much superior to that of the day before, I was seeking the Lord's guidance on the theme for the meetings. He showed me that He wanted us to have a communion service, so we stopped at a small town on the way and I bought a packet of wafer biscuits and a bottle of strawberry juice. 'Will I be able to take part in the service?', I asked Pastor Padua, knowing that in many places such a ministry was reserved to men. 'Of course', he answered, 'we of the brethren of Christ here in the Philippines have no prejudice against women.' He opened his Bible and read:

The Spirit himself beareth witness with our spirit, that we are the children of God, and if children then heirs, heirs of God and joint heirs with Christ.

Rom. 8:16, 17

Hallelujah! I could see that Jesus had accepted the women as joint heirs with Him, in the same way that He had accepted the men, for the women were as much a part of the church as the men were. I opened my Bible and read,

> There is neither Jew nor Greek, there is neither bond nor free, there is neither male nor female, for ye are all one in Christ Jesus.
>
> Gal. 3:28

I was greatly relieved by this attitude because I had an awareness that the Lord wanted me to preach on a theme new to me. It would have made it difficult for me, if the Lord were telling me to speak and the church was forbidding it, but I praised God for that Filipino church which really testifies to the truth that 'where the Spirit of the Lord is there is liberty!'

The demonic opposition to our presence in Palatong showed itself during the meeting on Saturday evening. The people were just getting used to Alex leading and beginning to join fully in worshipping our Lord and Saviour, when suddenly I began to cough and so did everyone else. I felt myself choking and I saw that everyone in the room was coughing and holding their throats. There was a rush for the door and as the room emptied I saw one girl, more affected than the rest, lying on the floor screaming; she looked as if she were having a fit. I ran over to her and began to pray in tongues. I could not understand what was going on, but the more I prayed in tongues for the screaming girl, the easier my own breathing became. I looked round; apart from one or two who had remained with me to pray for the girl, the room was empty. She was becoming calmer and her breathing was returning to normal. The cause of the problem was something in the air, which now seemed to be clearing. I could hear shouting coming from outside, the tones of a man in a fit of rage. The language barrier made it impossible for me to understand what he was saying but there was no mistaking the venom in the voice.

One of the team came in to tell me what they had found. When they had rushed out, they were confronted by a man armed with a rifle screaming curses and obscenities at them and blaspheming the name of Jesus. He was so beside himself with rage at the strangers who had come to the church, that he wanted to drive them out like wasps from their nest. He had ground up some dried pepper and wrapped it in cloth, which he set on fire and tossed into the building. The smoke from the burning cloth dispersed the pepper through the room with very painful effect, particularly to those with respiratory illness. The shouting was still going on outside and there were evidently spiritual forces at work, using that man to unsettle us and even kill us. I told those who had come back inside that the Bible said that Jesus had given those who follow Him power and authority over all devils. I said 'Father, in the name of Jesus, we take authority over the demons of darkness that are ruling in this man's life and command that they desist from trying to disrupt this meeting'.

Within half an hour the air had cleared, the man had left without using his rifle and the meeting resumed as if nothing had happened. Perhaps it would be truer to say that because of what happened, the Lord truly blessed the church that day. They were believers and loved the Lord but had not up until then understood what the Bible said about the baptism of the Holy Spirit. I explained that they had received the Holy Spirit when they believed but Jesus had promised more than this. He had told his disciples that they must wait to be endowed with power from on high (Luke 24:49). This promise had been first fulfilled in the Upper Room in Jerusalem at Pentecost and repeated many times, as Luke described in the Acts of the Apostles. It would also happen today, because Jesus had said that He would give the Holy Spirit to those who ask Him. Most of them asked, and we laid hands on them and heard many of them speak in tongues immediately.

On Sunday morning, the little church was packed for their first celebration of Communion. It was a first for me too; I had not ministered Communion before nor spoken on the everlasting covenant. As always, I looked to the Lord to fill my mouth and guard my tongue. I had been looking to Him for direction since I had known we were to have this service, but it was not until two minutes beforehand that the Lord caused me to open my Bible and my eyes fell on a Scripture that I had not noticed before:

> But I say, that the things which the Gentiles sacrifice, they sacrifice to devils, and not to God: and I would not that ye should have fellowship with devils. Ye cannot drink the cup of the Lord, and the cup of devils: ye cannot be partakers of the Lord's table, and of the table of devils.
>
> 1 Cor. 10:20–21

I had barely finished reading the Scripture when I realised that Pastor Padua was introducing me to the congregation. I started to walk across to the lectern, and in the few seconds it took me to get there God had revealed to me that there were some present who were involved in making sacrifices to devils. The church was very quiet as I started to speak, even the children ceased fidgeting on the hard benches. There was no mistaking the presence of the Lord. Words that were not prepared were pouring out of my mouth, coming from the Spirit of God who dwells within me. '. . . You cannot partake of the cup of the covenant, then go and make sacrifices to other gods, for there is only one true God, the maker of heaven and earth, who came in the form of

Jesus Christ and shed His blood to pay the price of our sins. The sacrifices which you make to your so-called gods are actually sacrifices to devils. Repent of these evil practices and God will forgive you. If you are involved in such practices, come forward and renounce them now.'

I waited, believing that the Holy Spirit would give them understanding of what I had said and would convince them of the seriousness of this sin. Two people got up and walked out. I waited; I was sure this would not be the only response, God had not brought me there for that! A moment later, a man and a woman stood up and moved forward and then from here and there in the congregation a little group assembled. Each individually renounced his worship of idols and the practice of making sacrifices to devils. We prayed and set them free by the authority of the Word of God and the power in the name of Jesus. They sat down, and again words came from my mouth, as I lifted up the cup, 'The wine in this cup represents the blood that Jesus shed at Calvary. If we confess our sins, He is faithful and just, and will forgive our sins and cleanse us from all unrighteousness. He will forgive your transgressions, He will forgive even the vilest offender who comes in true repentance. Let us stand before the Lord and confess our sins'.

The presence of God was awesome as we came before Him. Many had tears in their eyes; even the children were deeply moved. 'Now come and partake of the cup, in faith, knowing that the precious blood shed at Calvary has blotted out these sins forever. Put on the robe of righteousness and know that you are a child of the everlasting covenant and be confident that He, who has begun a good work in you, will perform it until the day of Jesus Christ.' Then I lifted the wafer and again the words came 'This bread represents the body of Jesus that was beaten and lashed for our physical benefit and by whose stripes you were healed. Believe the word of the Lord, partake of the bread in faith. As you do, the healing power of the Lord will flow through your body, causing your body to come into line with the word of God.'

So, one by one they came forward, and all who partook of the covenant with no wavering, left the Lord's table clothed in robes of righteousness and healed in mind, body and spirit. Some fell under the power of God and the children were evidently affected by the powerful corporate anointing on the meeting. They were no longer looking at the adults and copying them but experiencing the presence of the Lord for themselves and worshipping from their hearts. After this outpouring of God's love, which created new bonds between us, it was hard to leave next morning, but I felt drawn to visit Palasaan before returning to Baguio for the start of the second phase of our mission.

Palasaan was a tiny village perched on the edge of a deep canyon, where a few mining families lived in isolation, having little contact with the outside world. Each morning, the men of the village descended hundreds of feet to the bottom of the canyon, from where the sloping shaft of what had once been a productive gold mine tunnelled into the base of the mountain. I had found this out-of-the-way place, or rather the Lord, who loved these people, had brought me there, on my previous visit. They had heard the Gospel gladly, and some had been born again, at that time, so when, after a hair raising journey, I arrived for the second time on the canyon floor, I was met with big smiles and warm handshakes. They were all anxious to tell me that the Lord had answered my prayer of five years earlier and they had found a small vein, which had yielded enough gold to repay their labour. We gathered at the shaded side of the canyon and worshipped and praised God together and I spoke to them about the one true God and his son Jesus. They had a new problem in the mine, they said: would I come and pray? A miner carrying an oil lamp led the way into the tunnel and we all followed the flickering light. We rounded a bend which shut out the daylight, and the darkness, after the glare outside, was impenetrable. The floor was rough and in places, where the tunnel was only three feet high, we had to drop to our hands and knees and crawl. To add to the discomfort, water dripped from the roof and ran in rivulets along the floor. Here and there, a wooden prop had been inserted to hold up the roof and as we groped our way round these, I could not help feeling how slender they seemed, compared with the weight of the mountain. Then we reached the problem; the flickering light was reflected from a pool which stretched away into the darkness. The mine was flooded and they had no pumps to remove the water. So we prayed for the safety of the miners and asked the Lord to drain away the water, then we turned and began our crawl back into the light. There was much handshaking and some shy attempts at thanks from these men who saw few visitors and were clearly moved by our having taken the trouble to seek them out again. For me, it was a reminder that the Lord's plan was that the Gospel should be preached to every creature, before His return. He knew where they were and would bring His good news to the ends of the earth.

Chapter Fourteen

I awoke with a tremendous feeling of anticipation, for today was the day when I would start out for Kalingo Apayao. That was the province where, five years earlier, a Filipino pastor had looked at me inquiringly and asked 'Why have you come?' and even though I had to admit that I did not know why I was there, he had said, 'We have been praying for a missionary to go to the headhunters!'

Go to the headhunters we did, and they responded, as people everywhere do, to the love of Jesus. Now God was bringing me back to go to other, even more remote villages, but first we had to get one hundred and eighty miles to the north of Cruz La Trinidad. Pastor Padua reckoned that the journey would take us fifteen hours and he was concerned that we should not be on the road very late at night. So he had ordered an early start. We had packed the night before; Marilyn had been up even earlier to ensure that we had a good meal before we set out. By five thirty while it was still dark, Alex and two men from Pastor Padua's church had arrived to join us. The jeep from Miracle Mission, which was going to take us all the way was expected at any moment. We knew that they had intended to start out at three thirty to tackle the steep forty mile drive from San Fernando, on what was a relatively good surface, but the hours went by without a sign of them. By eight o'clock we were becoming concerned and considering going down to the telephone exchange as soon as it opened to telephone them. At a quarter to nine they arrived, to our great relief, safe and sound. Loren was driving and Pastor Abe was sitting in front. In the back, Darella, her two children, a boy aged seven and a girl of eleven, and Betty Dahl were sitting, surrounded by all the electrical equipment. 'Sorry to have kept you folks waiting, but we had to turn back', said Loren, as soon as the jeep rolled to a stop. 'We realised that when we packed the generator and lights we forgot the amplifier.'

'Well we're certainly glad to see you looking in good shape', I said, 'Can you fit us all in?' We arranged ourselves quickly on the seats, legs intertwined with baggage, and were soon on our way. I had travelled this route once before and the road was no better than I had remembered it. Although it was the only route north through the centre of the country, the road had lost most of the tarmac it once had, and as Pastor Padua had foreseen, we managed less than 20 mph. Although we were trying to press on to cover as many miles as possible in daylight, at one o'clock we simply had to find a drink and a comfort station (a euphemism for a very smelly tin hut, having no door, enclosing a hole in the ground, not convenient but very public!). When we stopped, Betty, in her rush to get there, tripped in a pothole. She did not hurt herself but when she straightened up and dusted herself down, she looked round to find herself surrounded by grinning children who had seemingly materialised from nowhere to see the discomfiture of this 'big Americano lady'. Having found an object of such rare occurrence, they were not going to miss the next episode and when she did not trip up again they followed her into the comfort station. They paid no heed whatsoever to her pleas, that they should go away. In the end, she was forced to recognise that there was no help for it and her dignity would be better sustained by ignoring them, than by further cajoling!

By nightfall, we still had about fifty miles to go. Pastor

Abe had taken over the driving from Loren, whose eyes were aching from the day-long glare to which they had been subjected since dawn. A fresh pair of eyes were needed, because we were soon to turn east off the main road, such as it was, on to a dirt track which would take us the final miles to Tabuk. Our progress slowed, and without the cooling air flow through the open sides of the jeepney, we began to feel hotter than during the middle of the day. This was not helped by the cloud of dust inside which we now travelled, and which quickly coated our hair and faces so that in the dark all we could see of one another were the whites of our eyes and an occasional glimpse of teeth! By now everyone was feeling tired and conversation languished. Darella's children were leaning against her, dozing despite the jolts, Alex, who frequently cheered us up by starting to sing, decided instead to inject a very gloomy note into the silence. In his broken English, or rather, broken American, he said, 'Very dangerous just here, sister Isabel. Much NPA hanging around. Bad place for ambush. Nobody rides car here at night, too much frightened of kill and rob.' So that was why, since darkness fell, ours was the only vehicle on the road; I was glad that I had asked the Lord to surround and protect us. Betty leaned over and whispered with a note of anxiety in her voice 'I wish he hadn't told us that.'

Then on that deserted road, the headlights of an approaching vehicle appeared, climbing up the hill behind us. It was moving faster than we were and would soon overtake us. Conversation stopped. Everyone retreated into his own thoughts. If the local people were so terrified of venturing out at night, who were these? Benighted travellers like ourselves? Or cruel killers, with a much more sinister purpose, moving under the cover of darkness? Had we been marked as an easy target at the last place we stopped? How should we react if they tried to block our path: crash through or abandon the jeepney and run for it?

If they knew the area and had lights and guns the chance of escape seemed slim. The anxiety we had felt since darkness fell was now giving way to a paralysing fear which was trying to grip us and take over our wills to stand against its source. In this kind of situation national characteristics show. The Filipinos stayed quiet; Betty was quite open about her fear and at the same time tried to make light of it. This became more difficult as the other vehicle inexorably closed the gap. Then it slowed to our speed and stayed just behind us. I could feel the tension rising. Only Betty managed to speak, 'What do you think they will do to us?' At that moment I had the oddest reaction. I started to laugh; Betty and Darella joined in, and soon, the Filipinos were laughing too. I had sometimes seen sad people at a meeting start to laugh, when I prayed with them, as the power of God fell on them. Now in the jeepney we all had the Holy Ghost giggles, and we were lifted above the fear of the situation. After about ten minutes we heard the engine behind rev up and a pick up truck with a cover over the back drew level, then passed us. We could not see who was inside. I watched with relief the rear lights disappearing around the next bend. Again Betty spoke the thought that niggled us all, 'Do you think they have stopped up ahead to set up an ambush?' And again the Holy Spirit enabled us to laugh, to laugh with such freedom from fear that tears ran down our cheeks making streaks in their dusty coating and our sides ached. We never did see them again. As the lights of a town came into view, we praised and thanked God, who had answered our prayers and kept us safe on this perilous journey and brought us to our destination.

We had arrived at Tabuk, the administrative centre of a region of the same name, where we were going to stay the night. It was the only occasion during my visit when I sampled a country inn. It was ten o'clock when we arrived, a late hour for country folk, but the lights were still on and loud music was coming from one of the windows. We found a compound where the jeep and its contents would be safe. Like ourselves the bags were thickly covered in dust and we had a quick brush down before entering the inn. I took an instant dislike to the place. We entered through the front room which was the one communal room for the guests and a drinking den for the locals. A lot of drunken men were staggering about talking very loudly and a group in the corner were arguing noisily and looked as if they might erupt in a fight. Half a dozen teenage girls were ranged around the room, unattached, leaning against the walls, looking as if they wanted to be picked up.

There were three bedrooms available, so all the men shared one, Darella and the children another and Betty, Lisa and I had the third. It had been a very long day and we were weary from the uncomfortable fifteen-hour drive, but before we could contemplate going to bed we had to get clean. We found the washing facilities in the basement. The basins were so filthy that my stomach heaved at the prospect of using them. Somehow, I had to get rid of the grime that caked in my hair and was ingrained in my skin. On the wall at waist height there was a tap. I felt I was being optimistic in turning it on but to my surprise clean cold water came out. I proceeded to have a stand up bath, still wearing my shoes to keep my feet off the dirty floor. After much scrubbing and rinsing and the expenditure of great quantities of shampoo and soap the last vestige of Highway 11 went down the drain and I was clean!

On the way upstairs we had to pass the drunks again, who seemed to wander freely around the inn with glasses in their hands. I saw the demons of lust looking out at me from their eyes and I rushed past ignoring their friendly gestures. Lisa followed a few minutes after me and a group pursued her upstairs and hammered on the door of our room. I shouted through the closed doors, 'Go away. We're tired'. 'No, no', came the answer, 'we like talk with you.' 'We are Christians, we have come a long way and we want to be left alone to sleep, now go away', I replied firmly. 'We Christians too, we come in, we talk some, Hallelujah, Praise the Lord, Amen' came the drunken reply. This time I shouted loudly enough for the team to hear, 'If you want to talk to someone, go and talk to Pastor Abe or Pastor Shields.' Through our closed door we heard the drunks being persuaded to go downstairs and we were not disturbed again. I was very glad to leave the place next morning, glad too, that we would not be staying there again.

Our base was to be at Laya, where Pastor Teckney lived in retirement, but on the way there, in accordance with the schedule we had prayed over together, we were to go to visit Bolo. Bolo was an easily accessible village about twelve miles from Tabuk with about two dozen dwellings of the kind which the Filipinos referred to as Nepa huts. They were built on a wooden framework with a thatched roof and had walls made of bamboo poles lashed together. There were Christians in the village, though as yet they had not erected a church or appointed a pastor. We were welcomed at the home of one of the Christians and the women in the team were able to relax as the men busied themselves, working out how to install the lighting. The electrical equipment had survived the trip without damage and, soon it was being erected around an open space in the village. Four stiff bamboo poles were set in holes at the corners of the site, a rope was then tied from one to the next and the lights were suspended from the rope. The generator was connected, and filled with petrol and started without trouble. The tubes glowed. They were of course quite insignificant in daylight, but I felt like cheering.

When it grew dark at half past six, an hour before the meeting, the generator was started again and the effect was dramatic. The space where the meeting was to take place stood out, the houses and trees were lost in inky blackness around and the light was drawing everyone to this great novelty. The adults would have seen electric lights in Tabuk, but to have it here, illuminating their own village was marvellous. The children went wild and ran in and out of the lighted area and then around the village calling their friends to come and see. So while we were eating the people were gathering not only from the village but from the scattered homes some distance away. Now I began to see one good reason why Jesus had instructed me to buy the equipment and how He was going to use it for His glory. Without it, there would have been no light; the light attracted the people, they would hear the truth and the truth would set them free.

This was to be Loren's only evening with us, so I was glad when he agreed to speak. Pastor Padua translated. He spoke simply about salvation and about the gift of the Holy Spirit. Many were added to the church that night and many spoke with other tongues. As in other villages, many of the infants and young children were sick and feverish and their mothers tended to be the first to respond, when we offered to pray for the sick. I believe all the babies were healed that night as well as some adults. Others were delivered from addictions to alcohol, tobacco and gambling. Our new microphone and amplification system helped us, because we no longer had to shout, and those who were healed were easily heard when they testified to what Jesus had done for them and their children.

When the meeting ended, we had to say goodbye to Loren, Dorella and the children, and Pastor Abe. No one wanted them to go and they would have loved to stay longer, but Miracle Mission had been functioning without them for two days and it would take them a whole day to travel back. They would be on the road before dawn and I greatly appreciated what they had done for us in undertaking such an exhausting two-way trip with just one day in between. We prayed for their safety and knew that the Lord would go with them and take them safely home. Betty and Lisa were going to stay for about a week with the team and I was grateful to have some female company.

When I was awakened next morning, by the sounds of the village coming to life, the jeepney had already gone and I lifted them before the Lord and thanked Him that He had heard our prayers last night and that He was leading them home safely. As the realisation that the jeepney had gone struck me it seemed that the dread of being stranded in a remote area with no transport and only a few pesos left in my purse had materialised. Pastor Padua had confirmed that he had not been able to make arrangements with anyone to pick us and the equipment up, but he thought there would be a jeep 'by and by'. This phrase, so often heard in the Philippines, might mean, tomorrow, next week or next month, so it gave me no confidence at all! So I rebuked all thoughts of the fear of being stranded and penniless and found a quiet corner where I came before God and reminded Him where I was and exactly what my financial position was and of the schedule I had agreed with Him two weeks before. As I did so, the peace of God flooded me and I knew He had the situation under control.

Later that morning, we had a most moving experience. Our hostess was trying to communicate something to me, which I was failing to understand, so I asked Pastor Padua to translate for me. 'She has a friend', he said, 'who lives outside the village. This woman is very sad because her small son died last week.' 'Is she a Christian?', I asked. 'Yes', was her reply, 'both she and her husband are Christians, but she will not come to the meeting because she is so sad. Please go to her home and speak to her'. Betty and Lisa came with me and when Alex saw us go, he picked up his guitar and came too. Pastor Padua was again our interpreter. We found the grief-stricken mother red-eyed from weeping and withdrawn. She did not respond at first but slowly began to tell us how much she missed her son, Gilbert. When we talked to her about Jesus, it was clear to us that she really loved the Lord and had been born again. She did not understand much more than that. She had very little knowledge of the word of God. The devil had taken advantage of their ignorance and attacked their child with disease, because they had not discovered that we must resist the devil in the power of Jesus' name and the devil must flee. They had not heard, so they could not know, that Jesus bore our sickness and carried our diseases and that by His stripes we were healed. In order to prevent Gilbert from further suffering, Jesus took his spirit out of his body and carried him to heaven leaving the empty shell to be disposed of, for God would one day give Gilbert a brand new immortal body, which would be incapable of decay.

With these thoughts running through my mind, I explained to her that the separation was only for a short time, and that one day, all who loved Jesus would be raised from the dead and spend eternity, which was time without end, together in the presence of the Lord, never to be separated again. We prayed that the Lord would comfort her and that she might know that what I had said was true. The Lord did a deep work in her heart and she was set free from grief, for she knew beyond doubt that she had an eternity to look forward to without tears and without parting. She dried her eyes, reached over and hugged me and looked up into my face with smiling eyes, a transformed woman. Her gloom and depression had lifted and she burst into activity. It was a time for celebration, a time to feast and rejoice, for her son was in heaven, forever safe in the presence of Jesus. She ordered their fattest pig to be killed and firewood to be gathered and soon the smell of roast pork had set everyone's mouth watering. For the next two hours while the pig roasted we sang and worshipped the God who gives life to the dead.

After that feast, God was again prompting me to have a communion service. Indeed on looking back I realise that this was a pattern which the Lord led me to follow in every town and village where a suitable opportunity offered, because none of them had been introduced to the practice of the regular celebration of Communion. The Pastors with whom I worked and associated in the Philippines were men and women anointed and appointed by God. They worked under extreme hardship, hiking into remote areas on foot, many times risking their lives to bring the Gospel to primitive tribes. I never discussed with them why they did not establish the communion service in these new churches. I can only guess that it had something to do with the fact that their converts had, in the past, been involved in heathen sacrificial rites so that they needed grounding in the Word, before they were introduced to the everlasting covenant, in order that there would be no confusion with their past pagan practices. If this was the case, it would fit with the Scripture which the Lord had given me at Palatong and which I continued to use when I taught on the covenant. Again at Bolo, I stressed that we could not drink the cup of the Lord and the cup of devils. That night the brethren believed and understood that all our needs were met through the blood and body of the sacrificial Lamb of God, Jesus.

I chiefly remember that evening for the children and young people. I ministered to them individually as they came to receive and ensured that they asked Jesus to forgive them the naughty things they had done and to understand that His blood was shed for them, that He loved them and had forgiven them. I explained that His body had been beaten and lashed so that they could be healed, and would never need to be sick. As I looked at the row of beautiful brown faces, looking up at me, with eyes full of love and trust, my own heart melted with love and compassion for them. Even though they were dressed in rags, they were princes and princesses for whom God had laid up a great inheritance. I said to them 'This bread represents the Body of Jesus, which was lashed, marked and disfigured so that you, a child of the everlasting covenant could at all times walk in divine health'. As my words were repeated by my interpreter their gaze moved from my face to his. As they partook of the bread in complete trust, the healing power of our covenant God was made manifest. In that quiet moment, the power of God came upon them, they fell to the ground and began to speak with other tongues as the Spirit of God gave them utterance. All who were sick were healed.

There is something special about ministering to children. They are precious to the Lord and He wanted His little ones to understand what He had done for them and that as long as they believed His word, they would never need to suffer disease and pain.

After another long day we were ready for bed. Betty, Lisa and I had been given a room with three Filipino plank beds on whose unyielding surface we arranged the air mattresses we had brought, then crawled under the mosquito netting and settled down. Before dropping off to sleep I dreamily wondered how the Lord Jesus was going to get us and our equipment out of Bolo and back to Tabuk. Six hours later, I woke with a start. Through the dawn sounds of cocks crowing, firewood being cut and the clatter of metal rice bowls, which had become so familiar, came the foreign sound that had jerked me awake. A motor vehicle was entering the village. I could hardly believe my ears, the Lord's provision had arrived even before I was awake. We threw on some clothes and rushed out. There standing on the track leading into the village was an ancient, beaten up, rusty jeepney. Pastor Padua had got there even quicker and when I arrived, he was negotiating the hire of the jeepney to take us to Laya, near Tabuk. I could not follow the dialogue, but the driver had clearly started from a very high figure and Pastor Padua was slowly but surely bringing him down. I wondered if it would not have been better that we Westerners should have kept out of sight since my presence would signal to the driver an above average ability to pay. How wrong he would have been! Pastor Padua told me what they had agreed and I turned out my purse. I had only one third of what was asked, but immediately Betty and Lisa came to my rescue and contributed one third each. The jeepney was carrying a load of provisions purchased from the market in Tabuk by various villagers, who busied themselves unloading sacks of green beans, bananas and even live chickens. The men of the team had already dismantled our lights and had everything ready, wrapped in polythene to protect it from the dust. It made a neat compact load and soon was all stowed. I was somewhat apprehensive when I clambered on, to find I had to step over holes in the floor, which felt as if it was about to give way wherever I placed my feet. I wondered if it would stay together long enough to get us to Laya. The others were praising God for providing this well-worn transport. I felt guilty about my thoughts and asked the Lord to forgive me. and of course, because it was God's provision, it carried us safely, without any trouble to our destination.

Pastor Teckney and his wife were living in retirement in the same comfortable house which I had stayed in five years earlier. With mattresses, running water and electric light, it was positively luxurious after the Nepa huts. Our arrival was a red letter day for the family; they were full of memories of our earlier adventures together and recalled little incidents I had almost forgotten or been too involved to notice. Tall for a Filipino, and most remarkable in that country for his neat military moustache, Pastor Teckney looked even leaner than I remembered and was just as gentle and quiet. But I sensed a note of sadness in their manner and conversation, that evening, and wondered what was disturbing them. It became clear next morning when we sat down to discuss our itinerary. His brother-in-law had been brutally murdered by members of the Bute-Bute tribe less than a year before. 'Sister Isabel', he said, 'Things are worse than when you were here before. We went then to the edge of the Bute-Bute area and we came back alive. You are talking of going right into their area. I tell you it would be suicide, you would never come back alive. The New People's Army have been getting rifles from abroad and have recruited many of these wild tribesmen and armed them. Nowadays there are army checkpoints on all the roads into the mountains from Tabuk so the headhunters don't remove a head any more, it is too difficult to conceal. Today they cut off their victims' ears, or fingers, and bring them back to their village as a trophy. There they are hung from the branches of a tree. The party is then joined by the rest of the men in the village in a pagan sacrificial dance around the tree. My own brother-in-law's body was hacked to pieces and his fingers were taken away. But now, as well as the tribesmen, there are the members of the communist NPA who are hiding out in the mountains and they finance themselves by robbery, kidnapping and ambushing vehicles. They hate Christians, especially Protestants and have murdered pastors in the northern part of Kalinga Apayao province. Even here, an area close to Tabuk, people are frightened to leave their homes after dark. It is because I fear for your life that I tell you these things, we all love you very much and want to protect you. Even if you could penetrate as far as Tulgao, it is most doubtful if they would allow you to speak in the village. None of us have been there and they are very suspicious of strangers and, of course, we don't know what language they would understand, we probably could not interpret for you'.

I listened without saying anything. I could see the effect that his brother-in-law's death had produced and how he could not bear the thought of a repetition. His description of the situation, though not news to my companions, had clearly shaken them. As I watched them nod in sympathy and agreement, as he was speaking, I felt my own resolve slipping. Yet I was sure God had pulled me back to this place, and we had prayed over every step. I excused myself to go and pray. Behind the house, I found a wicker hammock slung between two palm trees. I climbed in and lay quietly, meditating on the words I had just heard. Was I being stupid and foolhardy? Would we really be risking our lives by going into the mountains? Could we communicate with the people and would they listen? Most importantly, was it God's will that we went into the mountains? I needed confirmation from Him. I prayed, 'Lord I don't want to do anything stupid, most of all I don't want to bring harm to my companions. Please reveal to me your will in this situation'. I opened my eyes and looked up, waiting. The fronds of the palms were silhouetted motionless against a cloudless sky. Nothing stirred to spoil the tranquillity of that moment. It was hard to imagine that the people in this area lived in such fear that they would not venture out of their homes after dark.

The still quiet voice of the Holy Spirit spoke to my spirit and said, 'Are you willing to lay aside all for my sake?' 'Yes, Lord', I replied. 'Are you willing to lay down your life for my Word's sake?' I thought of Paul who had been lashed with thirty-nine lashes on five occasions. I thought of Stephen, being stoned to death. I thought of all that Jesus had endured so that a sinner like me could be set free from the penalty of sin. 'Yes, Lord, I know that your grace will be sufficient for me'. The voice of the Lord came a second time: 'I am asking of you complete commitment to me. Anything fractionally less than one hundred per cent commitment is not enough for my purposes. Through you, my light will reach out into the darkness of this world, in which you find yourself. There is no time to waste and you have no reason for delay'.

There was no doubt, it was the will of our Father that we should go. I was so relieved that the answer was so clear that I disturbed the peace with a loud 'Hallelujah'. I went to my room and wrote down the words which the Lord had spoken to me. When I came into the living room, where the team was still sitting, discussing the dangers, I sensed that fear was beginning to overrule faith. I read the words which the Lord had spoken to me; they accepted it totally, and at once the Holy Spirit moved in the hearts of the whole team. Lisa began to weep. Her break from school was almost up and she was due to go back to America. Yet she had formed such a bond with us that she wanted to come and share the dangers. The others found it less easy to weep but the Holy Spirit was giving each one a new love for the Father and for one another that opened up the way to complete obedience and trust. Betty too, had to leave soon to return to her responsibilities in the orphanage at the Miracle Mission but first we planned that she and Lisa would stay with us for just two more visits to villages near Tabuk, one of which was more primitive than any we had visited before.

Chapter Fifteen

The jeepney might have been a time machine so successfully did it transport us back through the centuries in a mere thirty-minute drive. We had arrived at a high flat bottomed valley, bright green from the rice pushing up in the paddy fields, with wisps of mist still floating around the tops of the palms. 'This is as far as the jeep can take us' said Pastor Padua pointing ahead to where the track ended against the retaining wall around the nearest field. 'We have to walk from here, but it's not far', he ended cheerfully. 'Look, you can see Epil'. And there it was, a cluster of huts on a sort of island in a sea of rice, the pointed roofs, at this distance, looking like sails of boats that had moored together for mutual shelter.

We had made a late start. Pastor Padua had spent the morning in Tabuk to arrange transport and returned in the early afternoon with a jeepney, into which we quickly loaded the lights and ourselves and got under way. The benefit of the delay had been a rain shower during the morning which damped down the dust, and we were able to travel without the usual cloud. When we got ourselves and the equipment off, the driver turned around and hurried back to Tabuk; he had made it quite clear that he would on no account wait for us after dark. Pastor Teckney, however, had assured us that there was a Christian household in the village who would welcome us. There was no road, not even a track into the village; no wheeled vehicle had ever disturbed its isolation. The only approach was on foot along the narrow tops of the walls separating the flooded paddy fields. These were slippery from the recent rain and the penalty for falling off was to sink deep into the mud among the rice plants, and suffer being attacked by leeches which abounded there. The men had to get not only themselves to the village, but also the equipment which they carried on a long pole laid on their shoulders as we progressed, in single file, towards the huts. Perhaps it was a good idea, after all, that we were not to return that night. I would not have relished that walk in the dark.

We found the Christian family, who welcomed us as Pastor Teckney said they would, and were happy for us to set up the lighting in front of their house. While the men hurried to erect the lights before night fell, Betty, Lisa and I walked around the village. The huts were built on stilts lifting the living quarters six feet above the damp ground. The space underneath was used for storing firewood and any livestock, usually chickens and often a black pig or two. Here, too, the poles and mortars used for pounding the rice, and the flat baskets for winnowing were stored. Everywhere the cooking pots were simmering and the smell of wood smoke was drifting out of the doors and window openings. Clothing was not a high priority need in their climate; the children ran about naked and barefooted, the women sitting in front of the houses, out of the smoke, were bare-breasted, the men returning from the fields wore only a G-string. With our interpreters all busy elsewhere, we could only communicate with nods and smiles and handshakes. A few backed indoors when they saw us coming, some others ignored us but most returned our greeting and shook hands. I had a strong sense that we were on enemy territory, spiritually speaking that is, so I prayed in the Spirit as we walked around, believing that we were 'more than conquerors through Him who loved us'.

When we returned to where the men were working on the

lighting, it was already growing dark. They had erected the lights on poles as usual, but the generator, which had started so easily before, was now refusing to go. We had brought small battery torches in our packs, and by their light the men checked again but could find no fault. The devil, our old enemy, was trying to prevent the evening meeting from taking place. We came against those demons of darkness and commanded, in Jesus' name, that they stop interfering with the generator. Another attempt was made to start the engine with no success. Jesus, when faced by the devil, had appealed to God's word, and it occurred to me to do the same. I shouted, 'It is written, demons of darkness, you must obey the name of Jesus'. The men tried again and the engine burst into life. The lights came on but then began to flicker on and off. The men ran around, checking the connections; they would get one to come on steadily then another would go out. It was as frustrating as the affair of the paraffin pressure lamp on my last trip. Once again we had to stand against our enemy and persevere until all the lights came on steadily.

It was eight o'clock before we started the meeting, much later than suited village folk, but the sight of the illumination and the sound of singing and Alex's guitar soon began to draw them. A steady stream of men, women and children appeared from the darkness to squat on the ground and listen and even attempt to join in. About forty people had gathered by the time I got up to speak to them. I depended entirely on the Lord to give me the words that He wanted the people to hear. I began, 'The great God of the universe, the one and only true God, who created you, has sent me here to Epil, from the other side of the world to tell you that He loves you and to reveal to you His ways.' A few wandered off again into the darkness but the rest listened with rapt attention about God's way of salvation through the sacrifice of Jesus, and when I asked them, nearly all wanted to turn to Him, so we led them in the prayer of repentance and salvation.

One of the team told me that there was a lad in the meeting who was totally deaf in one ear and had only slight hearing in the other. I called him up and someone near him, prodded him and pushed him up to the front. He was a bit scared at finding himself face to face with a strange white woman and I don't think he heard a word the interpreter said. Nevertheless, I spoke to him, and of course the congregation heard. 'The story I told about Jesus is true and I am going to pray to Jesus and Jesus will open your ears so that, when I finish praying, you will be able to hear'. The people who, up to then, had sat well back from me, now overcame their shyness and pressed forward to see if what I had been saying really was true. When they were quiet again, I spoke to the spirit that was blocking up his ears and commanded, in Jesus' name, that it leave the lad instantly. I yielded my voice to the Holy Spirit and as I prayed in tongues, the Lord performed a miracle. Someone clapped their hands sharply and he spun round to see what it was. There was a cheer from the congregation. Someone else got him to hold his hand over the ear in which he had partial hearing and found that he could repeat words spoken to him. The lad's demeanour completely changed, he was now not only healed, but he was a celebrity, demonstrating to everybody that he could hear perfectly.

While all this excitement was going on and attention was focused on the lad, a young mother carrying a tiny baby, came up and signalled by holding the back of her hand on the baby's forehead that it had a high temperature. She looked at me with great pleading eyes, and indeed the baby was in a bad way, lying very still in her arms and barely breathing, and its forehead when I laid my hand on it was burning. Once again I looked to Doctor Jesus, the greatest physician. When I finished praying the mother touched the child's forehead; it felt just the same and I saw a look of great disappointment in her eyes. I said, through the interpreter, 'Please don't worry, Jesus has healed your baby'. She wandered away and disappeared into the darkness.

Our hostess gave us some thick black coffee and we settled down with her and her daughter on the bamboo floor of the little Nepa hut. In the 10 feet by 10 feet space, four adults and four children somehow found enough space to stretch out and sleep. But there was no lying in! The rule had to be one up, all up. As we said goodbye to our brothers and sisters in Epil, they extracted a promise that we would return before we left the area and it seemed right to me to agree to that, though quite when it was going to be fitted in, I was not sure. Pastor Padua and the other men in the team had also been up early and quickly had the equipment ready to move. We retraced our steps across the paddy fields and found our transport waiting, two scooters fitted with sidecars. 'Fine' I thought, 'Wonderful that they are here waiting, but how are the other ten of us going to get home?' But I underestimated the Filipino talent of making do with whatever was available.

Pastor Padua took charge. He installed four men inside one sidecar, seated two more on the pillion and told a seventh that he had better perch on the back of the sidecar where the equipment had already been secured. Betty and I stood back in amazement as the outfit slowly moved off, then, as the rider got the measure of its balance, he opened the throttle and went bumping down the track, rounded the bend and disappeared. Now it was our turn! Betty was cast in a rather bigger mould than the average Filipino, nevertheless, she, Lisa and myself were somehow shoehorned into the sidecar and the two men climbed on the pillion, sitting sidesaddle. It was like no other ride I had ever experienced. Sitting close to the road one was conscious, in a wholly new way, of the size of the potholes and the force with which we were hitting them. But we survived and got back to Laya intact. I found afterwards that Pastor Padua had actually selected the scooters rather than a jeepney, because he had observed that my funds were getting low and scooters came cheap!

Chapter Sixteen

Betty and Lisa had time for one more visit before they would have to return to San Fernando; Betty to take up her duties at the mission and Lisa to fly back to America, to college. Sukbot was near Tabuk and was a village very like Epil, but it had an active church. I had visited it five years before and had been prevailed on to purchase a Nepa hut which was vacant and which I had left in the care of the church. Pastor Padua told me, that this turned out to be a heaven sent provision for a friend of mine. Her name was Pastora Carmen. I had spent a wonderfully fruitful week with her in 1981, when she was the pastor in the beautiful village of Lewan and had got to know her and appreciate her commitment to Jesus. Now she had transferred to Sukbot and it made me happy to think that my rather reluctant purchase was of service to her. We spent a busy day with her at Sukbot and again my main meeting was in the context of the communion service. I shared with her our plans to go higher into the mountains, beyond Lewan. She too, warned me about the dangers but encouraged me, when she saw I was resolved to go.

Next day, Betty and Lisa's bus from Tabuk to Baguio left at the unsociable hour of three thirty in the morning. No jeepney driver could be found willing to turn out after dark to take them to the bus station, but eventually a friend of Pastor Teckney's who had a car agreed to come out from Tabuk to Laya at two thirty to take them. We all went to bed early and got up at two o'clock to have breakfast with them and see them off. But we waited in vain for the transport and having sat around the kitchen table drinking coffee for two hours, Betty and Lisa had given up all hope of catching the bus, then the electricity failed. We did the only sensible thing, undressed by candlelight and got back into bed. We were just getting pleasantly comfortable when the noise of the car's arrival made Betty and Lisa leap out of bed and dress, in the hope that somehow or other, the bus had been delayed and they might still catch it. But the car's driver brought the news that it had departed on schedule and he admitted sheepishly that he had not woken up in time. So back we all went to bed yet again. However, to make sure that there would be no repeat performance, Betty and Lisa arranged to spend the next night in Tabuk and we saw them off that afternoon. They had both, with great kindness, emptied out their purses keeping only enough for their bus fares and gave the rest to me. I was going to miss their companionship.

Philip and Sheila White's arrival was imminent. They had never been to the Philippines before, and because I knew they would be carrying video and sound recording equipment in addition to their personal baggage, I had felt we ought to try to meet them. Betty's husband, Stuart, had offered to drive down from San Fernando to Manila and bring them back to Miracle Mission. Pastor Padua would take the bus from Tabuk to Baguio, another from Baguio to San Fernando and would return with them by bus to Tabuk. That was the plan, but, even with Betty and Lisa's gift, I did not have enough money for Pastor Padua's bus fare to San Fernando, and while our Father continued to ensure that we always had enough to eat, now I badly needed money, quickly. I had a cheque book with me and I expected that there would, by now, be some money in my account in England. However, I knew that banks in the Philippines took enormous precautions against cheque fraud. They would never part with cash against a cheque drawn on another bank until they had cleared it. From past experience, I knew that this took about thirty days. So I cried out to my heavenly Father, 'Lord, please touch the heart of the bank official in Tabuk, so that I can cash a cheque on the spot'. The bank official, to which the Lord led me 'just happened' to be a born-again Christian and when I introduced myself and told him of the need for money, he cashed the cheque there and then. I praised the Lord; He had yet again met with us at our moment of need. Pastor Padua caught the next bus south and had time to call in at Cruz La Trinidad to assure Marilyn that all was well, before going on to San Fernando.

I was glad to have a few days rest from travelling to catch up with washing and ironing and to have some time to read and meditate on the Word. On the second day, Pastora Carmen came down from Sukbot for a more extended period of fellowship than we had been able to manage when I had visited her village. She was about my own age and had pastored newly founded churches in a number of remote villages away from all the amenities of civilisation. As we talked, I could not help but be impressed by her faithfulness; she never complained about the harshness and deprivation of the conditions under which she worked. Her concern was for the spiritual welfare of the people for whom God had anointed her and called her to lead and teach. We spoke further about the plan to go deeper into the mountains and she listened and asked questions about the way God had been leading me to go there. Later the same day, she came to me and said, 'I have been thinking and praying about what you said this morning and I believe the Lord wants me to go with you.' I was deeply touched by her willingness to come. She, more than most, would appreciate the dangers and discomforts of the mountains, but I wanted to be sure that she had considered it carefully. So I said,

'You already know that Pastor Teckney has strongly advised us to stay away from the mountains; have you faced the fact that we could be killed?' Her reply was comprehensive and final, 'I am willing to lay down my life for my Lord as He laid His down for me. It would not be the first time I have faced death for the Gospel's sake.' She said this in a matter-of-fact voice, with no hint of boasting or self congratulation and went on to tell a remarkable story.

'In Sukbot, one evening we were in church', she began. 'How long ago?' I asked. 'Few months', she replied, then went on, 'I was Pastora and in front facing everyone. We were praising the Lord, in the Spirit, my eyes were shut. I did not see him come in. I did not hear him, nothing until he grabbed me by the hair. I opened my eyes. I saw a young man, who was drunk, with a bolo'. 'What's a bolo?' I asked. 'A bolo is a heavy knife, for cutting open coconuts, this long' she replied separating her hands to indicate about eighteen inches. 'His face was full of hate and he pulled me towards him by my hair and lifted the bolo to strike me. He brought it down with all his force on my neck then on my arm and then across my back. Even though the bolo was sharp enough to cut right through my neck and take my head off my body, God was with me. There was not one mark on me. My flesh was not even bleeding. He was amazed, he was afraid, he dropped the bolo and ran out of the church.' Pastora Carmen and her congregation fell on their faces before God and thanked Him for His mighty intervention, which had saved Carmen from sudden death. They took authority over the demons of darkness that ruled through the body of that young man and commanded in Jesus' name that they loose their hold on him. They prayed and interceded for the young man's salvation.

Later that week, the young man sent a message to say that he wished to speak to the Pastora. She agreed to see him and welcomed him without hate or recrimination. His name was

Eduardo and he had been born at Tulgao, a village deep in the mountains. His father was an alcoholic and at an early age, young Eduardo developed a liking for the local rice wine and would join in his father's drinking bouts, whenever they could get a supply. His father would become argumentative when drunk and a quarrel would start. One day, the quarrel developed into a fight and Eduardo, almost equally drunk, picked up a bolo and killed his father. When he realised what he had done, he ran away from home and wandered from village to village, until finally settling at Sukbot. The hideous memory of that final quarrel stayed with him. He could not live with the fact that he had murdered his father and was rapidly becoming an alcoholic himself, in his attempt to blot out the recurrent nightmare. He explained, that on the night that he had attacked her, he had been drinking and a voice in his head said, 'Take your bolo and go and kill the preacher woman'. He had struck at her hard enough to hack her in pieces and when he found her still standing there unhurt, he knew he was up against a supernatural power and was frightened. As he confessed this to Pastora Carmen, the Holy Spirit was at work in his heart and he was a completely broken man who through his tears, asked her to forgive him. Her heart was full of compassion, and she told him that she had already forgiven him. She told him that it was even more important, that he should confess his sins to God and that if he did, God would forgive him, for Jesus' sake. He there and then submitted his life to the Lord. He joined the congregation at Sukbot and showed a willingness to learn. However he still had trouble handling alcohol and his violent temper would occasionally flare up. 'You may not remember, Isabel', she went on, 'but he was one of the men who came forward for prayer when you visited Sukbot last week. Demons were cast out of him and he is now enjoying a new peace in his life and is no longer drinking'.

Pastora Carmen indeed knew what it was to live alongside violent pagan people and I was very grateful that the Lord had moved her to come and that I would have a woman companion on the trek. The team gathered for a time of prayer and intercession that evening, as usual. An unusual outcome of our waiting on the Lord, was a clear word that we should inform the police of our planned visit to the mountains. Three of us called a tricycle taxi next morning and in obedience to this instruction went into Tabuk, from where police operations for the whole of the twin provinces of Kalingo and Apayao were controlled. Our request at the front office to see an official about our intention to visit the mountains was met by disbelief, then, when we insisted, there was some very rapid passing on of responsibility. No one was prepared to cope with interviewing and giving permission to this mad Englishwoman. In the end, we were told that we should see the Chief of Police who was in a board meeting and would be free in an hour. So we sat in the headquarters waiting room and prayed in the Spirit.

The police in the province were engaged alongside the army in actions against the rebels and many wore combat jackets and were heavily armed. The place felt more like a barracks than my idea of a civil police office. Eventually, an officer appeared, and said that the Chief was now available and would see me. I was ushered into a large inner office and found myself facing a brisk, alert, military-looking man in a smart green uniform. He looked down at the note which the officer had left. 'You are Miss Chapman? Why do you wish to see me?', he asked. 'When we were praying last night, God instructed me to inform you of our plans to go and preach the Gospel of Jesus Christ in the mountains of Kalingo Apayao.' His gaze moved from my eyes down to my feet and back again. His attitude was not friendly. Foreigners who came to this out-of-the-way part of the Philippines were generally up to no good and I suppose he was wondering what I really meant to do. 'Does your God speak to you?', he asked. 'Yes', I replied simply. 'Why did you choose to come to the Philippines?', he snapped. It was interesting that he asked the question in that way, because it allowed me to say, 'I did not choose to come to the Philippines, God sent me here'. This really perplexed him. Before he had time to ask another question, I began to share my testimony and tell him, that in 1981, the Lord had told me to give up my employment and sell all that I had and come to the Philippines. He listened with great interest. Just before I got to the point of telling him that he too needed to be born again, he stopped me with a question, 'What do you know about the NPA activities in the area you plan to visit?' 'Nothing', I replied. 'You know nothing about the NPA activities in the area?' he repeated in surprise. 'Are you aware that the mountains of Kalingo Apayao are not a safe place for a woman?' he asked and his tone was more friendly. 'I've been informed by my Christian brethren that this is a dangerous area', I said without embroidery. 'But you still intend to go', he said quickly. I wanted there to be no doubt in his mind about the basis on which I was going, so I said firmly, 'Yes, the Lord will go with us and protect us'. 'Can I see your passport, please?', he asked. He checked it over and handed it back with a smile. I was glad to see that smile; he was not going to try to put any obstacles in our way. He held out his hand and we clasped hands in a friendly handshake. He wished me well, 'I hope you will have a safe and successful tour; I will inform the check point police of your intended visit'. Hallelujah! What God accomplished in and through that interview I do not know, but I had done what he had asked of me. I was glad it was over.

We made our way from the police headquarters to the bus station to meet the service from Baguio on which we were expecting Pastor Padua to return with Phil and Sheila.

When the bus arrived without them, I was not too surprised. Pastor Padua had talked of trying to persuade Jacob to drive them up from Baguio and to stay in the north for a while, to transport the team. Pastor Padua told me later, that when he had arrived home, he had contacted Jacob and told him that he needed to go to San Fernando to collect two friends of mine and come back to Tabuk. When it came to negotiating the price, Pastor Padua had to admit that he had no money, but that he knew my friends would at least have money for petrol, so they could all get to Tabuk; then he hoped I would have some money to pay for the hire. Jacob must have had confidence that the money would be forthcoming, for he agreed to come.

So we went back to Laya and sure enough, late in the afternoon, Jacob's red jeepney rolled up to the front of the house. I was so glad that all the arrangements had worked and that God had brought them safely to us. In my relief and joy at seeing them, I laughed and they looked at one another and laughed too for they were disguised under a thick covering of dust. Phil's black beard was now grey as a badger and it was impossible to tell that Sheila was a redhead. 'I can't wait to get in a bath,' Sheila whispered as we embraced, and I broke the news in a whisper, 'We don't have baths here, but don't worry, we do have cold running water'. So we introduced Sheila to the pump in the yard and while Pastora Carmen worked the handle, Sheila got her head under the spout and in a scene that would have served for a television shampoo commercial, emerged with gleaming red hair. Her hair colour was a continuing wonder as nothing like it had ever been seen in Tabuk.

Sheila and Phil dusted down their bags and the equipment cases and brought them in from the jeepney. First to be unpacked was a large flat envelope addressed in familiar handwriting. It was from Ron, my helper and partner in Norfolk who had continued to look after my account and correspondence while I was away. The size of the sum of money that I pulled out of that envelope staggered me. We counted the high denomination notes and found in all one thousand pounds. I praised God for the way in which He had provided for our needs. I had spent one thousand dollars at His bidding and He had replaced it with one thousand pounds. We could now afford to pay for the hire of the jeepney, if Jacob was willing to stay for the next month. He felt a strong pull back home to be with his wife and new baby, but as usual, God had the situation under control and had revealed his purposes to Jacob. Before we asked, he had made the decision to be our team driver. My God never ceases to amaze me.

Next out of their baggage was a large parcel from my other faithful helper and partner, Daphne. It was a nostalgic link with Britain and home, for it felt as if I had been away for ages. So I attacked the parcel with all the eagerness and excitement of a child on Christmas morning. It contained thirty-seven separate packages and I reserved the right to open all of them! It was great fun. The first one I opened had a brightly coloured shirt which was just the right size for Pastor Teckney, next a bag of sweets, which we all enjoyed; Daphne's thoughtfulness had provided something for everybody in the parcels.

Next day we had kept free to give Phil and Sheila a chance to recover from their journey. They spent the morning unpacking and checking their equipment and found that it had survived the journey without damage. We were now fully equipped and staffed for our next outreach and it was an exciting as well as a solemn moment. The solemnity was much in evidence when Pastor Padua spoke before our evening prayer session. He said that no one was to embark lightly on this journey. It might cost us our lives, so if anyone was not sure that they were prepared for that cost, they should not go. It was better to stand down now, rather than to turn back when half way there. No one backed out. We prayed and asked the Lord to guide us, and to keep us safe by sending His angels before us to make the crooked places straight. We continued to pray in the Spirit for approximately two hours.

During this time the Holy Spirit moved upon Pastor Teckney and as he wept, he was set free from the fear for our safety that had been ruling his heart. Now he could contemplate our departure with joy, knowing that the good news of Jesus was being taken into new territory.

Chapter Seventeen

We went first to Lewan and then had planned to go directly to Sumadel and Tulgao but the Lord revealed that we were to fulfil our promise to return to Epil, especially to establish a spiritual leader and that we were to do the same at Bolo. Bolo was nearer and we drove directly there.

While we were praying in the pastora's Nepa hut before the meeting, we were interrupted by the sound of wailing and sobbing from outside. I went to the doorway and looked out. As soon as I appeared, a hysterical woman, carrying a tiny infant, ran towards me and thrust the baby into my arms. Someone translated the words coming through her cries, 'She thinks her baby is dying'. I looked down at the tiny face, its eyes were rolled back, with only the whites showing, I could see no sign that it was breathing. In the name of Jesus we rebuked the demons of darkness that were trying to take the child's life, knowing that they had to obey. We all yielded our voices to the Holy Spirit and prayed in tongues. Immediately, before our eyes, we saw the healing power of Jesus move in that little body. The baby began to breathe, irregularly at first, then more steadily. Its eyes were moving, colour was returning to its face and the fever was disappearing. I put the baby back in its mother's arms and said, 'By the Lord's stripes your baby is healed'. She looked down at the baby and saw that it was true. Her wailing stopped and now tears of joy replaced the tears of terror and she went away, clutching her child protectively to her bosom, to share the news with family and neighbours.

That evening, the Holy Spirit moved in a remarkable way and men's hearts were opened to offer themselves for the work of pastoring the church in Bolo and the Lord showed us the man He had chosen.

Next morning, before we left, I went to call on the mother of the baby who had so nearly died the evening before. I found her sitting in her hut, nursing her baby, who showed no trace of illness and was feeding happily. I did not interrupt but went quietly away thanking Jesus for the healing that He accomplished long ago.

A man from the congregation sought me out during the morning to tell me what had happened to him, when I had been there three weeks before. He said that for six months, he had suffered severe pain in his head and in his stomach. As it got steadily worse, he thought that he was going to die and the only solution seemed to be to leave Bolo and seek hospital treatment in town. He was told that the cost would be two thousand pesos, or about a hundred pounds. He had no money so, on the day before he was due to set out, he went to a moneylender and borrowed it, at an interest rate of ten per cent a month. That same evening he came to the meeting. 'I want to tell you what happened', he said, 'I heard you say that Jesus was beaten so that I could be healed. When I understood this, and rebuked the devil in Jesus' name, I was healed, and the pain went and did not come back. I never went to town and was able to give the money straight back to the moneylender. I was very glad because I did not know how I would ever have repaid it.' We rejoiced together, and both of us agreed that Doctor Jesus was the greatest Physician, who gave all his blessings free of charge.

We got away by noon and called back to Laya to see the Teckneys. We were welcomed in to clean up before setting out, later in the afternoon, for Epil. Sheila had been badly bitten by mosquitoes again and we persuaded her to stay behind and rest and pray, while we were at Epil. Jacob dropped us off, and hurried back with the jeepney to the safety of town.

Our return to Epil enabled me to enquire about the baby we had prayed for on the night the deaf boy's hearing was restored. I was told that the baby was alive and well and that its mother would be at the meeting that evening. So before we came to the selection of a pastor for the church, she testified that the Lord had healed her baby as I said He would, though she did not see that the fever had gone till the following morning. After I had spoken and we had prayed together, there was unanimity in the church that God's choice to pastor the flock at Epil was Valentino Oplay. But the choice was made in his absence. His wife explained to us that, when he had heard that we were going to Sumadel and Tulgao, he had been prompted by the Lord to offer his services as guide and interpreter and had already set out to meet us there. Pastor Padua was greatly encouraged by this news, because Brother Oplay travelled extensively in the area in connection with his job, and knew the tracks and could speak many of the dialects. Where it had seemed impossible at one time, that we should ever find a guide, the Lord had now provided two!

Preaching and ministering at Epil was much harder than it was, for example, at Lewan, and though the Lord manifested His power in healing and deliverance, I felt all the time, that we were up against powerful spiritual opposition. I was exhausted, physically and mentally. Pastor Padua was tired, too. Only Phil looked his usual cheerful self, as he busied himself filming around the village. They both came and prayed that the Lord would strengthen my weak body. By the grace of God I hiked back over the paddy fields and was very glad to see Jacob and the red jeepney waiting.

We had a day's rest at Laya before going on. It gave us the

opportunity to sort out our baggage so that we only took the minimum for the long climbs ahead; the rest including our passports and money we left with Pastor Teckney until we returned. To reach Sumadel meant a long drive to Banghad, and the certainty of delays on the way at the checkpoints. At the first one, we stopped at the bamboo pole which barred the way and the corporal in charge made us all dismount and searched through our equipment to ensure that we were not carrying military supplies. When he had satisfied himself that we were not NPA, he signalled to his men who lifted the pole and waved us through. We had no further delay at the later checkpoint.

Banghad was the largest town in this area, and the point from which we would begin our climb to Sumadel. One of the local people, who knew Pastor Padua came to me and said, 'Why are you passing us by? We would like to hear you speak in our town.' I explained that we were going higher up the mountains but that if they would arrange a meeting for the day we returned I would be happy to speak to them. Sadly, this did not happen because the local Roman Catholic priest did not approve of us. We parked the jeepney outside the police station, shared out the loads to be carried, donned headgear in a range of styles and set out.

Chapter Eighteen

Sumadel, hidden away in the mountains of Kalingo Apayao, was a village which might well have been described as 'off the beaten track'. But it was a very well trodden path, which we took from town. It was just wide enough for us to walk in single file, the men laden with the equipment, which would enable Philip to make this first ever film record of Sumadel. It was one of the stiffest uphill routes we had tackled and as we left the dappled shade of the jungle and emerged on the edge of the treeline, we were exposed to the full force of the tropical sun. The glare was frightening in its intensity. I rummaged in my bag and found sunglasses and pulled on again the big floppy straw hat which had been hanging round my neck. I could now look away over the plateau, from which we had come, to the encircling peaks. They dominated the landscape making trees and rocks and the villages, which were dotted here and there, look puny beside their towering massiveness. I thought of the majesty of God who created it all and that even the earth itself was only a speck in His vast universe. And as we toiled on and up, He sent a breeze, which set the tall pampas grasses rustling and cooled our perspiring faces. Here and there, water flowing off the mountain had turned the path into a slide, up which we struggled. 'I'm afraid,' said Pastor Padua, 'that the last kilometre is the worst. When I was here in December it was very steep and slippery.' But a surprise awaited us. We found that a long flight of concrete steps had been installed! Not, Pastor Padua reckoned, by the Highway Authority but by the combined labour of the men of the village, who would have carried the cement up from the road on their shoulders. The steps took us to the summit of the hill on which the village was perched, overlooking the paddy fields, which had been constructed wherever there was an extensive flat area.

The village itself was amazing. Its four hundred houses were crowded as close together as if the land was as valuable as Mayfair! Perhaps in their terms it was; in spite of their primitive way of living they were now connected to the money economy. I was told that to buy a plot and build a house with a galvanised iron roof would cost eleven thousand pesos, about six hundred pounds. How anyone there could hope to amass such a sum I never discovered. Before a hut on the rugged hill top could be built, a level area had to be created by building dry stone retaining walls. When I went visiting, I was continually scrambling up and down over seemingly endless stone walls. The reason why the villages did not spread out was the wish for mutual protection. 'Not that it is necessary today because of the peace pact', Pastor Padua explained. 'Tulgao and Dananao have always been enemies and their fighting would sometimes spill over into Sumadel. There is no head-hunting because of the pact. However, if it is broken the head-hunting will start again'.

Pastor William confirmed this, as he took me round the village. The people of the Sumadel region had not been head-hunters for many years but had often suffered at the hands of neighbouring tribes who were. Nor had the people taken much interest in the NPA. Peace had helped the church to take root. It had been established there three years earlier and William was the first pastor. I never did discover his second name, so I got in the habit of addressing him with what the Filipinos probably thought was an improper informality, as Pastor William. He had been born in Sumadel, but spent some time in town, where he had gone to school and learned to read and write and to speak very passable English. He was a quiet, godly man who found it difficult to know how to relate to me and especially to the camera, but the love of God 'which was shed abroad in (both) our hearts' broke the barriers of race and culture. There were now more than one hundred Christians in the village, he told me, and I believe they were sufficiently numerous to be influencing the morality and prosperity of the place by their witness and their prayers. Three years previously, every house had its idols and charms and an altar or shrine at which they worshipped. Now paganism was in retreat before the Gospel and it showed in a desire to change every aspect of their lives, in cleanliness, in wearing clothes, even in learning to read and write and in getting free of addiction to alcohol and tobacco.

In spite of the fear of the NPA and the limitation that this placed on movement around the tracks and roads after dark, the people of Sumadel regularly trekked to town, to sell their produce and buy what they could not produce. This brought the Christians into contact with longer established churches and among the things which they had brought back were the words of songs in English. So when they had children's Sunday School in the open air, I heard with delight them singing 'We are gathering together unto Him'.

There was no church building in Sumadel, and it was difficult to see how they could hope to build one without outside help. For the present, they held their meetings in two rooms of an ordinary house. When I stood up to speak, not only was every inch of floor space taken up inside, but people surrounded the house to hear the message coming from the loudspeakers and pressed in at every window opening. The heat from all those bodies and the lack of ventilation added to the already high natural temperature. Before long we were all mopping our brows and leaning heavily on the Lord's grace to ensure that we did and said what He wanted, and did not allow circumstances to prevent us. For the later meetings, as the numbers attending grew we moved into the open air. Every day the Lord added to the number of the Body of Christ, and in obedience to the great commission the new converts went through the waters of baptism.

I was conscious, in the days spent at Sumadel, that I had arrived after that long, hot, uphill walk, feeling tired, and that I was steadily becoming more drained. The spiritual battling, the unaccustomed physical hardship, changed diet, the heat and the lack of sleep were taking their toll. It was impossible to get a full night's sleep in a village geared to awaken at four thirty in the morning. I was rarely able to get to bed before midnight as ministry to individuals could carry on long after the meetings ended. I was sleeping in a room with six others and at first light, the cocks would crow and the dogs would start to bark, the piglets would join in with their high pitched squeals. Then it would be the babies' turn. All four hundred houses in the village seemed to have babies in them and they would start to cry. The bamboo walls and the open windows shut nothing out. The babies would waken their mothers and soon they would be calling on the older children to get the fire going and pound the daily supply of rice. Then the steady thump of a hundred mortars would inform the world that the village was awake and functioning. By this time, my Filipino companions would be stirring and further sleep would be impossible.

Late one afternoon, when it was time to change for the evening meeting, I felt so exhausted and weak that I thought my reason was going and that I was about to crack up. For just about six seconds I thought I was going mad, I just could not cope with the situation for another second. Those six seconds were the worst moments of my life; I fell on my knees before Jesus and yielded my voice to the Holy Spirit. The Spirit of God took my voice and began to intercede on my behalf. I was aware that I was crying out in the Spirit and became oblivious to my surroundings. The whole village must have heard my cries, but that did not seem to concern me. I had reached the end of my self and, to be able to continue, I needed Divine intervention. For about half an hour the Spirit of God cried out on my behalf. During that time, Jesus performed a miracle in my mind and in my body, because suddenly, I knew it was over. I had broken through to knowing that I was able to face whatever lay ahead. Hallelujah! God's grace was sufficient for me.

Phil and Sheila too, I knew, were also under strain. Phil had been very sick after a meal of fish and crabs eaten at Lewan. Sheila had red blotches all over her body where she had been badly bitten by mosquitoes and other insects. Around her ankles the bites had become infected and pus was oozing out where her shoe had rubbed during the long walk up. She, too, overcame by praying in the Spirit.

Some members of the congregation at Bolo had come up to Sumadel to join in the meetings and were followed, a couple of days later, by Brother Valentino Oplay, who expected to surprise us; instead we surprised him, by telling him that we believed he was God's choice as pastor at Epil and had the support of the men in the congregation. Brother Oplay completely agreed with the advice which we had already received from Pastors Padua and Teckney, that only a small team should go to Tulgao and that no cameras or recorders should be carried. We had to avoid doing anything which would raise suspicions that we were spying on them, otherwise we could be shot on sight. So we decided to abide by the plan that had already been worked out. Pastora Carmen and I and five of the men would go on, and Phil and Sheila would return to Banghad with the others, where Jacob would be waiting to drive them back to Laya. They would collect all the baggage that had been left at Pastor Teckney's house and return and pick us up when we got back from Tulgao.

Chapter Nineteen

Flickering pine wood torches lit the open space between the wooden houses. The evening breeze came in little puffs, stirring the flames for a moment to chase away the shadows and reveal the grey stone walls bounding the area. Now and then, the glint of metal reminded me that the men sitting on the walls at the edge of the crowd had automatic rifles slung over their shoulders. Behind them, the comings and goings of the mountain top village were lost in the inky blackness.

The trek up here to Tulgao had been the longest and most difficult yet. We had retraced our steps down from Sumadel into the valley in the dawn light. In the cool stillness of the early morning we struck a good pace downhill and across the rice paddies in the valley. An hour later we were facing the slopes of the next range and when we paused for a drink from our water bottles, Eduardo said, 'We must cross this mountain, there is no way around'. We followed his pointing finger to where a path zig-zagged out of the trees and across the bare summit. It turned out to be a very irregular rocky track, sometimes squeezing along narrow ledges with long drops into the valley, on one side; in other places it traversed deep cracks on a bridge made of a couple of bamboo poles. When we reached the summit, we could look away across the next valley to where Tulgao sat on the top of the next range. At that distance, the thatched houses and their unpainted timbers merged so perfectly into the background, that I could hardly pick them out. There was still a long way to go and after six hours on the march, I was already struggling to keep up. Eduardo was anxious to reach our destination in daylight and pressed on at a pace which soon neither I nor Carmen could match. The muscles in my back and legs became so weak that my steps were shaky and uncoordinated and I had to stop. The consequences of not being able to go on, and being stuck in this area, were too desperate to contemplate.

I prayed, asking Jesus to renew, restore and strengthen our weak bodies and I yielded my voice to the Holy Spirit and prayed in my heavenly language. I felt the power of God surge through my body and instantly the trembling in my legs stopped and they became strong again. Carmen was also refreshed and strengthened at the same moment and we were able to speed up. By now, the sun was high in the sky and out of the shade it was blazingly hot; our clothes were soaked with perspiration and sticking to our bodies. Once again, I found myself crying out to the Lord for help to endure the heat. When we paused for a rest and a drink, Brother Oplay saw how much the sun was affecting me. He tried to encourage me by saying, 'Just another hour and the greatest heat of the day will be over'. We got on our way again and after ten minutes he turned to me and pointed to the sky. 'Look', he said 'God has brought a cloud'. I watched and saw the cloud move to cover the sun. Tears filled my eyes; I was overwhelmed by the presence of Jesus. In that otherwise cloudless sky the hand of God had formed and moved a single black cloud to overshadow us. At the same moment I felt the air stirring and then a delightful cooling breeze surrounded us with a feeling of freshness.

It was still daylight as we approached the village. We had been in full view of their lookouts for the last hour. I wondered what kind of reception committee would be waiting for us. Eduardo and Oplay went in front with Padua, Carmen and myself close behind. We waved and smiled. Women, bare-breasted, with babies slung on their backs, men, many of them wearing only a G-string, were moving out from the houses to see the white woman. There was not an armed man in sight. I looked into the faces staring at me and I saw only curiosity. The men who were speaking to Eduardo and Oplay were even getting excited. They translated for me: This was a special occasion. No white woman had ever walked all that way to visit them before. They wanted to show their appreciation by having a feast. They would sacrifice a pig as a thank offering to their gods, then they would bang on their sacred gongs to summon up the spirits and perform their victory war dances.

I was prepared to cope with hostility but what did I say to this? If we went along with it, in the interests of harmony, the place would be full of demons; we would be associated with worshipping them. Even if there were time left for preaching the Gospel, they would be in no state to hear. It was as well that I had been given that commission from the Lord which adjured me not to worship nor to sacrifice to their gods but to utterly conquer and break down their idols! It was a delicate situation. I relayed these thought to Oplay, and prayed that God would give him the words. He told me afterwards what he had said. 'This white woman has travelled a great distance, thousands and thousands of kilometres, in one of the great flying machines which you see in the sky. She has come especially to tell the people of the mountains about the one and only true living God. She is only here for a short time. If you have a sacrifice and dance she will go away to the next place and you will not have heard the good news she has for you in Tulgao'. Those whose taste buds were already savouring the rare taste of roast pig and the excitement of the dance, took quite a lot of persuading. I was aware that, in parallel with Brother Oplay's negotiation, an unseen spiritual battle was being won by the prayers and authority of all those believers in

Britain and the Philippines who were backing us up with their intercession. Finally they agreed, and showed us the open area betwen the houses where we could hold the meeting. Eduardo introduced us to his family and they prepared some food for us.

We rested, looking out over the most magnificent mountain vistas I had ever seen. Out there, I knew groups of NPA soldiers were training and waiting for the moment of revolution but in this village, at this moment, God was waiting to change men's hearts by His Spirit. By this time the adults had drifted back to their houses to prepare the evening meal, but the children remained, inspecting me from a safe distance; when I looked back at them they would giggle in embarrassment and pretend to play a game together, before pausing to scrutinise me again. Carmen looked at me. 'Do you think I should try to teach them a chorus?' she asked. 'It would be a very good place to start', I replied. She gathered them together and began to teach them to sing in English. They caught on very quickly and were soon doing the actions as well. Eduardo and Oplay were going round the houses making sure the whole village knew that the white woman was ready to speak to them. They slowly assembled and sat around, gently puffing at their clay pipes, looking to where I stood. We lit the paraffin lamp and switched on the battery operated loudspeaker. Darkness had fallen. Latecomers arrived bringing flaming torches which they inserted in the cracks in the wall. By their light, I could look into nearby faces. Those at the back blended into the shadows. They were all waiting for me to speak.

For a moment I was lost, not knowing where to begin, as the realisation hit me with fresh force that I was speaking to many people who had never heard the name of Jesus. I knew that they were animist, that they understood about demons and about someone Eduardo referred to as the Red

Devil. Was that a place to start? As these thoughts ran through my mind, I realised the futility of trying to work it out or do what I had previously done when faced with this situation. 'Lord', I prayed, 'I don't know where to begin, please help me.' I opened my mouth in faith and once again the Lord took over. I can only describe it by saying that He took my voice and spoke through me. Oplay interpreted for me and I found I was talking about salvation. 'God so loved the people who live in the mountains of the Philippines that He gave His only begotten son so that if the people here would believe in Him they would not perish but have everlasting life.' I described what perishing meant and told them that they had to turn from worshipping idols and sacrificing to demons and make Jesus their Lord. When I began to tell them that it was shameful to bow down to idols and that they should destroy them, I heard voices raised in opposition. They objected to their gods being brought down.

As the clamour rose from the darkness all around me, I thought of their rifles and, for a moment, my voice faltered. The devil took the opportunity to throw one of his fiery darts into my mind, 'If you open your mouth and speak another word you will be shot dead.' I glanced at Oplay; he gave me an encouraging smile. 'Oh well', I thought, 'if I'm going to be killed, I'll go down preaching.' The moment of fear passed. I was able to proclaim the word with greater freedom and authority. A new emphasis was apparent in Oplay's voice too. A few minutes later, we were interrupted by a noisy drunk, who staggered into the space in front of me, shouting at the top of his voice. I heard the members of the team, who were sitting behind me, begin to pray in the Spirit. The Barrio captain got up, took the man by the arm, calmed him down and persuaded him to sit quietly. All eyes turned back to me and I continued, telling them of God's love for them and the authority which He gives to believers so that they have power to stand against the devil. I gave them testimony to the times here in the Philippines I had seen Jesus deliver people from evil spirits, heal their sickness and take away their addictions. I ended by calling on them to turn from their gods, who were no gods at all, and submit their lives to the only true God, Jesus Christ. I stood there, not daring to say another word, waiting for a response. A holy hush had descended on the crowd. Minutes passed. Then the Barrio captain stood up and walked towards me. I held out my hand and he clasped it in a warm handshake. When I looked up, another five men were walking slowly in my direction. My eyes filled with tears, but tears which were the overflow of a thankful and joyful heart, that these men were stepping out of darkness into light to the glory of Jesus. The other members of the team took over and ensured that the men understood what they were doing.

Carmen and I were given a room in the Barrio captain's house and in a moment we were sound asleep, too weary to even think about the dangers. Our plan was to be up at first light to return through the mountains to keep a rendezvous with Jacob and the rest of the team. We were keen to be on time, so that they would not have cause to be concerned for our safety. But we were not to get away so quickly.

Pastor Padua woke us at half past four, while it was still dark. Pastora Carmen got busy and peeled some sweet potatoes, blew the embers of the fire into life and made some chips to have with our thick black coffee. As we ate, the Barrio captain came to share with us his wonder at what had happened the previous night. Eduardo interpreted what he said for me. Normally the village was a very wild place after dark. The men would come back from work in the rice fields and start drinking their home-brewed rice wine. After an hour or two, drunken fights would break out and the peace of the village would be shattered by cursing and shouting. It had become much worse since the NPA had distributed rifles because now they fired into the air to add to the din. Worse still, if they got into a drunken rage over gambling losses, they would shoot at each other. He was therefore amazed at the peace that ruled in the village since we arrived; there was only one drunken man. Only God could do such a thing.

As we sat listening to the Barrio captain, the man who had been drunk walked in. Pastor Padua and Oplay began to talk to him and translate enough to help me keep up with the conversation. He turned out to be the head of the spiritists in the village but was an alcoholic. He had invoked and sacrificed to the spirits to free him from his addiction but they had not helped him. He turned to me, 'Can the God you spoke about make me free from it?' The men explained to him in his own language, that an evil spirit wished to control his life, through alcohol. If we spoke to that demon, and commanded it to leave him in Jesus' name, it would have to obey. They went on to tell him, that they would not cast the demon out of him, unless he was willing to renounce his idols and his spiritism and accept Jesus Christ as the only God in his life. If he did this, Jesus would fill him with the Holy Spirit, who would enable him to resist the devil's temptations. The man did not want to renounce his gods, but he urged us to cast out the demon. Pastor Padua told him that it would be dangerous for him if we did as he wished, because there was the possibility that seven more demons would come and he would end up seven times worse.

I had long ago learnt that the fact that people lived a primitive life style did not mean that they were stupid. I got the impression that, despite his hangover, this was a highly intelligent man. He was also spiritually aware, even if his knowledge had all been gained on the dark side. He pondered what had been said, then got up and walked out. I looked at the others, wondering what was going to happen next. We did not have to wait long; in a few moments, he returned, carrying a bundle of tobacco leaves, which were a valuable commodity in Tulgao. But he still had questions and Pastor Padua patiently answered. He pointed at me, 'Why do you speak against drink? Father Gilbert, a priest in the lowlands, drinks, smokes and takes drugs. He is a priest and it can't be wrong if a priest does it?' I explained that we must be obedient to what the Bible says and not what the priest does. Finally, all his questions were answered and he got on his knees and said 'I am willing to try your God's way'. 'Are you serious?', Oplay asked. He threw his tobacco leaves on the floor and said, 'To prove to you I am serious, you can burn my tobacco.' He continued to kneel, as he watched it burn. He renounced spiritism, alcohol and tobacco. We laid our hands on him and cast out the demons of darkness in Jesus' name, and led him in a prayer of salvation. To God be the glory! Seven of the most influential men in the village were now filled with the Holy Spirit. Pastor Padua told them of his intention to return and they promised him a great welcome. We set off down the mountain rejoicing with the angels of heaven over the work which Jesus had done in the hearts of these seven.

Chapter Twenty

The sun was already up by the time we left Tulgao and began our long hike down to our rendezvous with the jeepney and the members of the party we had left behind at Sumadel. It was easier going downhill and we felt that there was less danger now from the villagers, though there was aways the possibility of bumping into a group of lowland NPA members hiding out in the mountains, who would not be sympathetic to our presence. At one point, as I looked ahead across a small valley to a path parallel to the one we were on, I glimpsed a man leaning against a rock with a rifle in his hand; when I looked up again he had gone and I never saw him again. But there was no room for fear to take root in my heart, as I rejoiced at the way that God had worked and the spiritual breakthrough that had been achieved with just one meeting. It was so obviously His power which had been at work and which had taken what we, in our weakness, had offered. I was lost in awe at the thought that God had taken us into His operations and manifested Himself through us and would continue to help us. The lighthearted way my companions were moving down the trail showed me, that they too felt the joy of His presence. No one had suffered so much as a bruise or a blister in either the hiking or the confrontation we had been through. So, in spite of our delayed start, we were at the rendezvous where the track joined a dirt road by three thirty in the afternoon, half an hour before the appointed time.

The jeepney had not yet arrived and, as we sat down to

wait, we realised that the long hike through the midday sun had left us hungry and thirsty, with our water bottles empty. When, at quarter past four, the jeepney still had not arrived we decided to continue walking down the road along which it would have to come. It was after five when we came to the first village, a little group of corrugated roofed huts with woven bamboo walls. The houses may have been primitive, but the villagers had hospitable hearts and when we asked to fill our water bottles and they realised how long we had been walking, they insisted on preparing a meal of rice and beans for the six of us. We were now beginning to feel anxious about the non-arrival of the jeepney. The local people told us that we could reach the next village on foot before dark and we decided to carry on. I was amazed that we had the strength to keep going, after the activities of the previous three days and the long hours on the track that day. Travelling around Britain in my Mini and ministering late into most nights was not the kind of preparation that made a body fit for long marches in the tropical heat. But here we were cheerfully setting out for another hour of hot dusty walking and singing praises to God as we went. It was a miracle.

Just before darkness fell, we heard the sound of an approaching vehicle and suddenly round the bend came an enormous dust cloud, at the centre of which we could see a red jeepney. As we recognised it as Jacob's, a spontaneous shout of 'Hallelujah!' from all six of us echoed in the trees and we began to shout, wave and jump up and down like children in the middle of the road. But there was no answering wave from the back of the jeepney as it screeched to a halt. A very dusty Jacob and Alex jumped down from the front seat and before I could ask any questions Padua got his in first, but in Ilocano. A long conversation ensued, of which I understood not one word! I was bursting to know where the others were, and why they had not come as arranged. Eventually, Padua explained to me what he had learnt. The effects of the rapid transition from Britain to the Philippines had caught up with Philip and Sheila. As they had turned out for the jeepney that morning, in Laya where they had gone the day before to collect our baggage, they were still exhausted and Sheila's fair skin seemed to have suffered much more than the rest of us from the bites of mosquitoes. The thought of a long, hard dusty drive after which they might not have much opportunity for filming had eventually persuaded them that it was better to return to Baguio and get fit for the next phase. It was good to know that they had come to no harm. But now the lateness of the jeepney meant that the meeting scheduled for that night was going to start late and therefore finish late. We piled into the jeepney, turned round and sped, as only a Filipino driver knows how to speed, and arrived at the end of the track leading to Mallango at a quarter past seven. By now the sun had set, but a bright moon lit up the rice paddies.

We squelched along the edges of the fields, the men carrying the generator, cables, poles and lights which Alex and Jacob had brought. God gave them the strength not only to maintain a cracking pace, but to get the lights set up and working in double quick time. As the centre of the village sprang into light, gasps went up from the villagers and soon everybody who could walk was gathered to enjoy the illuminations – Blackpool was never so attractive. The village children, rubbing sleep from their eyes were not going to be left out and heard me talk of Jesus who loved them and died for their sin and was inviting them to turn to Him for forgiveness and healing. Almost all the children in the village complained of the same symptoms of pains in their heads and chests. The Lord revealed to me that this sickness was due to the sins of the fathers passing on to the children. Generations of idolatry and paganism had brought it upon them (Exod. 20:5). After the parents had renounced these evil practices and accepted Jesus as their Saviour I was then able to cut the children free from these generation bondages in Jesus' name. It was two o'clock in the morning before the meeting ended and we switched off the lights and retired to the house where we had been offered a room. We had managed to have only six hours sleep in the last two days, so even though my air bed leaked and the bamboo floor was hard, nothing was going to stop me sleeping.

For the next week we moved down the dirt road stopping at each village to encourage the Christians and each night to hold a public meeting complete with illuminations, at which we saw the power of the Lord manifested to save, heal and deliver. To leave the mountain area in which we had been operating meant descending to Bontoc to pick up the highway. Jacob was apprehensive about this part of the trip because the road to Bontoc was the main access to the higher ground. That made it a favourite for NPA ambushes in which vehicles were hijacked and passengers robbed and murdered. It was also so narrow and winding that it was controlled at both ends to ensure that vehicles travelling in opposite directions did not meet. Local rumours hinted that the NPA had taken over the checkpoints so we prayed and asked the Lord to get us safely past these parts. It was a relief when we arrived at the first checkpoint to find that a Philippine army unit was in control and they waved us through without any delay. The same thing happened at the second and we were safely out of the mountains and out of the area in which the NPA were most active. We gave God the glory for our safekeeping in the previous weeks.

Highway 11, which runs south to Baguio through Bontoc is like the curate's egg, good in parts. It is mostly tarmac and is therefore an invitation to the driver leaving the side roads to speed up. At intervals, stretches up to a quarter of a mile long occur, where the top had been worn away leaving a deeply potholed road-bed often with large stones projecting. A pile of rocks or a few empty beer cans were the only warning to slow down before hitting these stretches. Jacob had now been along the road often enough to know where these were, but now and again as his concentration wandered he would enter one at sixty miles an hour. We would grab hold of anything solid to stay in our seat and groan at the bone-shaking jarring as we wondered how the tyres and steering could possibly stand up to the pounding. But they did and we arrived in Baguio, the northern capital, dusty but in one piece. The wives of the men of our team received their husbands home with joy and relief knowing full well the dangers they had faced.

As soon as I had washed, I hurried to the telephone exchange and went through the rigmarole of making an international telephone call. I filled in a form giving my name and the country and number I wanted to telephone and paid the fee for a three minute call. Then I joined forty or so other waiting people and as their names were called, they went into one of the eight cubicles, where they would then wait, while the operator tried to find a free line to Manila. Sometimes, the whole process had taken three quarters of an hour, but this time the wait was much shorter and soon I was speaking to Daphne and hearing that she was all ready to set out for Heathrow on the morrow and that she would bring with her six thousand pounds, which the Lord, through His Body in Britain, had provided to purchase a jeepney. Philip and Sheila celebrated our return by taking us all out to dinner. They insisted that I have a steak. It tasted indescribably good. As I shared with them the good news from Daphne we had a real celebration. Our anxiety about transport was over.

Chapter Twenty-one

'*A LAND OF CONTRASTS*', said the poster at the bus station, but I doubt if the writer had been exposed to the rapid changes I was experiencing. The previous night, after weeks of living off rice eaten in Nepa huts in primitive villages, I sat down in a pleasant restaurant and was served a perfect *filet de boeuf*. Today after long hikes on mountain trails, I was speeding in an express air conditioned coach the 150 miles to Manila. Up there in the mountains of Kalingo Apayao we had waited all day to see a single jeep, now as the coach approached the capital we were in a mad tidal wave of jeepneys, trucks, buses, scooters, motorbikes and tricycles rushing headlong with roaring engines and screaming horns to engulf Manila. When I alighted at the central bus station, the traffic smog was actually visible, reeking of diesel and exhaust fumes. Sumadel might have been on another planet!

I found a jeepney going in the right direction and arrived before long at the Manila Bible Training Centre. On my first visit to the Philippines, I had met Pastor Isaguirre, the director of the Centre, and he had asked that on my next visit I should speak there. I had written from England to say that I would be arriving on 28 February to meet Daphne and he had offered to drive me to the airport next morning. I was very pleased that he had, because I knew how useful it was to have someone who spoke the local language, if there were any bureaucratic snags at the airport. He welcomed me warmly and introduced me to his wife, who showed me up to their spare room, a great luxury in the Philippines! Over dinner, I told him about the expedition with his friend Padua and he got excited about how God had worked and said I must tell his students. 'But first', he said, 'you must get in touch with Pastora Solpico'. 'Pastora Solpico?', I said, 'Oh, you mean Susan!' 'Yes', he replied, 'she has telephoned a few times, asking if you had arrived. She has been very busy on your behalf!' I was intrigued; I remembered how she had enthused about meetings in Plaza Miranda, as I sat tired and jet lagged on the night of my arrival and the morning before I left for San Fernando, I recollected I had prayed with her and told her that I was not able to stay in Manila and help, but that she should go ahead as God directed. I wondered what He and she had been doing!

Next morning, with a heart full of joy and excitement, I met Daphne. She had had an uneventful journey and passed quickly through immigration and customs. As she mopped her brow in the sudden warmth after the air conditioned aircraft and arrival hall, she was looking me up and down. 'You've lost weight Isabel, and you look utterly weary', she said, 'you must rest.' As we walked towards the car park I protested that I was quite able to carry on, but no amount of arguing on my part would sway her; she insisted that I should have three days' complete rest. She turned to Pastor Isaguirre for a suggestion about where we might stay for three days and he immediately said, 'Open Doors', and went on to explain, 'It's a guest house owned by a missionary society in a pleasant part of the city. Let's go straight there and see if they have room.' The large house was beautifully furnished, with central air conditioning and nice soft beds. Outside, set in a garden of tropical trees and flowers, was a swimming pool. After six weeks in the mountains, it was like paradise. And, oh joy, they had a room with twin beds vacant. As I quietly thanked the Lord for his provision, Jesus spoke in my heart 'Because you have been faithful in proclaiming my word in the mountains, I will lavish on you good things'.

When Pastor Isaguirre had left we settled down to share the events of the previous weeks. Daphne had a wonderful story to tell about how the money for the jeepney had come in and I recounted some of the astonishing things I had seen God do in the mountains. After all that had happened, I found it difficult just to do nothing, to relax from that continual alertness to physical and spiritual danger and the readiness to stand up and proclaim the truth at every opportunity, as well as keeping track of time, distance, transport and money. I had always known that Daphne was a caring person, but now I saw what a perceptive love she had, as she gently persuaded me to switch off and enjoy the presence of the Lord, moment by moment. We swam in the pool several times a day and sat on the terrace for hours, reading the Word. Daphne went exploring in the nearby streets and found a restaurant, that served delicious food, where we ate each night to the sound of soft piano music. It was a much needed rest, before the six weeks of continuous ministry which lay ahead.

On the second morning there, as we sat at breakfast, I was aware of a telephone ringing, but paid no attention until the waitress came and said, 'Telephone call for Isabel Chapman.' I went to the telephone and heard Susan's voice answer my 'Hello?' 'Oh, Isabel, I have got so much to tell you. Do you remember I was to arrange some meetings. Well, God has done mighty miracles. I must see you tomorrow.' She sounded ready to explode with excitement. 'Daphne and I will be at the Bible Training Centre from tomorrow morning', I replied. 'Can you meet us then?' 'Yes', she answered 'but be ready for big surprises!'

We had scarcely settled in at the Bible Training Centre when she arrived, her dark brown eyes glowing with elation. She gave Daphne a long hug of welcome to the Philippines, then turned to me, 'Isabel, do you remember the day you arrived we discussed arrangements for a three day crusade at the Plaza Miranda?', she asked. 'Oh yes, I do remember and I'm sorry I could not stay to help you,' I replied. Susan hesitated, then said, 'Well, at first I wasn't sure if you thought it was a good idea, but you said to go ahead, and as soon as I did, I knew it was right.' 'Tell me what happened' I said. She explained that she had thought of the Plaza Miranda because she had arranged meetings there before, and knew the officials and the procedures for getting permission, and that it would not be too costly. She wrote a carefully worded letter to Mayor Begazzine, asking for a permit to hold a religious meeting with a visiting British evangelist, but felt nervous about going to present it at the Mayor's office on her own. She was an ordinary Filipino, without money, and needed moral support. She knew a Christian woman who was a solicitor, Fiscal Vita Villesina, and called round to her office. They spent some time discussing the arrangements which would need to be made for the crusade, and were just about to set off to the Mayor's office, when a policeman who had been talking to one of the clerks in the office, came over. He said that he had overheard their conversation and added very forthrightly 'It is not good to hold your crusade at the Plaza Miranda; the Quirino Grandstand is the right place'.

'Isabel, as soon as he said that, I felt in my spirit that it was right, that it was what God wanted, but I could hardly believe it was possible'.

The policeman explained that he worked with the management of the Quirino Grandstand to plan the policing arrangements for events held there. If she wrote a letter to the management, similar to the one for Plaza Miranda, he, Josef Lesago, would be the person to work it out.

181

'So I dared to say yes to him Isabel; I agreed, and it has come to pass by the intervention of God, that the Quirino Grandstand has been granted to us, free of charge. At first it was for one night only, but we prayed and went back and asked for three nights and they extended the permit.' She was ready to jump up and down with excitement and I looked at her enquiringly, not really knowing what all the fuss was about. 'You don't really understand, do you?' she asked. 'The Quirino Grandstand is the biggest outdoor venue in Manila, in the whole of the Philippines. It can hold a million people'. 'Surely not a million', I said wonderingly. 'Yes', said Susan; it's the place where the big political rallies are held and where the Pope spoke when he visited Manila.'

She had my full attention. I was beginning to catch her excitement, so I said, 'Just calm down, Susan, and tell us all that again'. By the time she had gone over the story a second time, I was realising, what a tremendous vision she had been given for our 'crusade', and the mighty things God was doing through her. But there was more. She continued, 'In all the preparations, God has guided me step by step. I had asked a few people if they knew a printer who was cheap and quick, but nobody gave me a name. Next day, a man called on the telephone; he said he'd heard I wanted some printing; he could supply posters in one thousand lots at two pesos each. This seemed very cheap, so I accepted over the telephone, but I had no money. During my prayer time, the Lord instructed me to go to San Fernando and tell Pastor and Mrs Dahl. They received me well and I explained the situation to them. They gave me enough money to start the printing. I got back to Manila as quickly as possible and worked out the layout of the posters with the help of my brother-in-law. I gave the printer a cash advance and told him I would pay the rest when you came. They trusted me and went ahead. I also thought we would need some banners, so I had some printed on cloth, long enough to stretch between telephone poles on the main streets'. I sat back in amazement at the effort she had put in for these three meetings. To her they were not meetings but a crusade, like the big American evangelists held. But they would send a large advance team to make the arrangements, armed with at least a hundred thousand dollars for expenses. Here was one Filipino woman, with no visible resources, doing the same thing.

'How many posters did you have printed?', I asked. 'Eight thousand in all', she replied. 'How on earth did you manage to stick up eight thousand posters?' I asked, while trying to imagine the size of the pile. 'Well', she said, 'we started with four thousand and it took several days; I had asked the people in the fellowship I belong to and young people from other churches and a lot of Bible students came out too, and we had several jeeps available. We actually worked all through one night. However, within a couple of days, many had been ripped off and thrown on the ground. The Lord told me to go back to the printer and order another four thousand. Since they still had the type set up, they did them by the next day. But this time I had a problem. Most of the people from the churches and the Bible schools were not able to come at such short notice and I had no transport. I turned from the telephone in tears, and cried out to God, Father, please provide a jeep or let me die tonight. The Lord heard my cry; the telephone rang and two jeeps were provided. When no Christians were available, God provided unbelievers. I just went out with a few friends in the two jeeps, late at night, and thrust the posters into the hands of anyone who would take them and told them to stick them up. Some had even come out of bars with bottles in their hands and were far from sober and between postings would have another swig!' She giggled. 'I did not criticise them, but thanked God for them. They did a good job and did not ask for any payment. When God has ordained something, no man can shut the door. I have also passed the word to the pastors and ministers of Manila and they are spreading the information through their congregations. Pastor Dahl is coming down from San Fernando with a group of students. He will be in charge of the music and two other groups, one from the Bible Training Centre and one from a local fellowship will lead the praise and worship and sing. Pastor Isaguirre is to be chairman and he has asked other pastors to join him on the platform. They are bringing men and women from their congregations to act as ushers and counsellors. A group of intercessors has volunteered to pray in the days leading up to the Crusade and during each meeting.' By the time Susan had finished, I was speechless. I was left in no doubt that God had ordained these meetings in a bigger way than I had ever thought, and I was part of it. I did not dare worry about it; God's grace would be sufficient to see me through.

Phil and Sheila had arrived from San Fernando that morning and were shown in by Pastor Isaguirre during the last part of Susan's account. 'The next thing,' said the Pastor, 'is to show you the Grandstand'. He drove us there and we walked on to the platform, which was big enough on its own to seat three hundred people. As I looked out at the vast concourse, all five foot three of me felt dwarfed by these surroundings. On three sides, of the platform a paved area stretched out for two hundred yards and merged into the grass of a large park. In the distance, the office blocks of the city could be glimpsed through the palm trees in the park. On the fourth side, behind the platform, was the Grandstand, from which the place was named. Was this all true or was I dreaming? I looked round, and knew it was real; knew that I had to face up to the fact, that tomorrow evening, standing on this very spot I would be proclaiming the word of God to hundreds, maybe thousands, of people.

We walked out on to the concourse, where electricians were at work; Pastor Isaguirre explained, 'The amplification and lighting have been loaned to us at no cost. I tell you God has arranged these meetings. Do you know that two television channels and one radio station are giving us free advertising. He is the potter and we are just little lumps of clay in His hands'.

There did not seem to be anything for me to do that afternoon, so with Daphne, I went off to buy a dress. I felt it would be nice to have a Filipino dress to wear for the first night, so Daphne and I prayed, 'Lord if it be your will that I have a new dress, please lead us to the one that you want us to buy'. Susan came round the shops with us to show us where to go. We had spent nearly two hours in different shops, but could find nothing suitable. I was just about to give up, thinking that if it had been in the will of the Lord, he would have led us to the right shop straight away. We came out into the arcade, intending to return to the Bible Training Centre, when two uniformed men came over and one said, without explanation, 'You must go to Tesoros', so I said, 'Where shall I find it?' He replied, 'I will take you'. I looked at Susan. 'It is a very expensive shop', she said, 'with lots of handicrafts; they do have Filipino-style clothes there too, I think'. The man led us through the streets, until we came to a large store. We soon found the dress department and there, in front of me, was a whole rail of lovely dresses, in just the colours I wanted; so many in fact, that I had great difficulty in making a choice. I picked out three, a blue, a beige and a red one, and took them to try on. They all fitted perfectly. I did not know which to choose, so I prayed, 'Lord which should I have?' Into my spirit came the words, 'You are a daughter of the King, you are a princess, you can have all three, one for each meeting'. I had to check myself, it sounded so much as if it were coming from my own wishful thinking; yet I had only hoped for one. As I still wavered, the shop assistant told me the price and said I could have ten per cent discount. The cost of the three then turned out to be what I would have expected to pay for one, going on British prices. I knew then, that the Lord was overcoming my natural carefulness because He wanted to show His love for me and give me all three. I thanked Him with all of my heart; I just keep falling in love with Him over and over again! I left the shop carrying my big parcel and the uniformed man appeared again. 'I see you got what you wanted; did they give you ten per cent discount?'. I nodded and passed on. We walked home, praising God, that even in this detail He was providing.

The following morning we gathered again at the Grandstand and were joined by Susan and Mahan, who was in the intercession team. Phil was setting up his camera and recording equipment. He needed a platform on which to mount his camera and the Grandstand staff could not find one which was the right height. Mahan began to pray, asking the Lord where she might find one. She set off in what she felt was the right direction and seeing a restaurant wondered if they might have a tall table which would do, but when she enquired, the owner was away and no one was interested. That was not where the answer was. She kept walking through the streets, believing she was led by the Lord at each junction. She saw a sign on a building 'Ministry of Public Works and Highways'. Plucking up courage, she went in, found her way to the man in charge and explained what she needed. 'We have four stands like that,' he said. 'Oh praise God!', said Mahan, 'Can we borrow one?' 'Yes', he replied. 'Oh praise God!', said Mahan again, 'And how much will you charge?' 'There will be no charge, and we have a pulpit you can borrow', replied the official. Mahan shouted 'Oh praise God!' She hurried back with the good news, and to make arrangements to collect the stand and pulpit. 'Do you need anything else?'

she asked Philip. 'Well,' he said 'the lighting that has been installed will be adequate for ordinary illumination but it is not really bright enough for filming. We could do with some more high intensity lamps.' Mahan was no longer surprised to find that the friendly official could offer her a choice of lamps, free, of course! Oh, Praise God.

The meeting was due to start at seven thirty in the evening and we arranged to arrive an hour beforehand. The helpers had put out five hundred chairs and when we got there all was in order, with ushers appointed to guide people to their seats and the musicians unpacking their instruments. I was praying in tongues all the time, refusing to allow my mind to dwell on the size and importance of the occasion, which could have made me anxious. Instead, I kept my thoughts on Jesus, knowing that as He had provided for our needs in the preparations, so He would undertake to do all that was necessary in the meeting. We joined the intercessors in the rooms at the back of the stage to pray with them until the meeting began. At seven o'clock, we walked out on stage to check how the seats were filling up. Stuart Dahl was playing the organ, but the whole scene looked desolate; there seemed to be no more people around than at half past six. I felt so disappointed. No one said anything, but I saw the same emotion in Daphne's and Sheila's eyes. 'Quickly, Daphne', I said, 'get everyone who is involved in the meeting to join me in prayer; musicians, singers, counsellors, everyone. Get everyone, who is not busy, to come here and pray'. She gathered together about a hundred people and our cries of intercession reached the throne of God. As we prayed in the Spirit, our faith and confidence was built up, and the realisation swept over us afresh, that the meeting was ordained by God and He would bring in those who had ears to hear. At half past seven, Daphne came back with news that the chairs were now filled and a steady stream of people were still arriving.

By now, I was remembering that no one in the Philippines expects meetings to start on time; to be half an hour late is to be in good time! We started the meeting at eight and two thousand people were present and more were still arriving.

The meeting began with praise and worship and soon this music-loving people were filling the stadium with their voices. It was marvellous to hear such a volume of praise rising up in the centre of the capital. I preached in English and had no need of an interpreter because in the city it is everyone's second language. I told them that God had provided completely for their salvation, that it was not to be obtained by good works but by faith in Jesus. The Lord led me to stress that He hates idolatry, that to bow before an idol was an act of worship, and all who continued to bow down to idols would be cast into eternal damnation. About one thousand people came forward in response to the call for salvation; it was the greatest demonstration of the work of the Holy Spirit, in convincing people of their need to be saved, and to turn from idols, that I had seen anywhere. I also felt that the Lord was leading me to do something I might normally have been hesitant about, when I had not taught about it. I briefly explained that Jesus, as well as being Saviour, was also the one who baptised in the Holy Spirit, I then led them in a prayer asking Jesus to do that. No one laid hands on them, but Jesus was not constrained and soon a thousand voices were speaking in tongues for the first time, as the Spirit of God gave them utterance. I then invited anyone who was suffering from any kind of sickness to join me at the front. People swarmed on to the platform from all sides of the concourse, and Jesus, the great physician, moved in our midst. Hundreds of people, suffering from many kinds of physical and mental disease, were instantly healed, delivered and set free from Satan's bondage. Words cannot express the awe and the joy we felt at being in the manifest presence of the Holy Spirit.

When the last person had been ministered to by the team, I left the platform with Daphne. As we walked towards the exit, she pointed. 'See that man over there who is folding up the chairs, just look at his face.' It was the face of a man of thirty-five, lit up with a smile which stretched from ear to ear; his face shone with joy. She went on, 'He had a tumour in one eye and had lost the sight of it, but Jesus healed him instantly tonight, and he can now see clearly with it'. He saw us approaching and came over to tell us how the Lord had saved and healed him. I left the park, with the joy of that man setting the seal on a remarkable evening.

I woke the next morning with a sore throat and a voice reduced to a whisper. Since I believed, that as a child of God, I had a right to enjoy divine health, I rebuked the evil spirit who was attacking me, in Jesus' name, and reminded all the forces of darkness that the meetings were ordained by God and there was nothing they could do to prevent the word going forth. I was a little hoarse at the start but my voice did not weaken through the evening meeting which incorporated a communion service. Daphne estimated that three thousand people came forward to receive the bread and wine, in a long line which took two hours to pass in front of the platform. The good humour and patience of the Filipinos was evident in that there was no grumpiness at the end of this mighty queue. They sang, praised and worshipped as they waited, led by the music group on the platform. They came, understanding the truth that the bread did not become the body of Jesus nor the wine His blood, but they just represented the body and blood of Jesus, and this truth set them free. Jesus commanded that we were to do this in remembrance of the sacrifice that He had been for us. I had proclaimed that those who had truly repented and received Jesus as Saviour and Lord were children of the new covenant and as they partook of the bread and wine, by faith in the completed work of Jesus, they would receive the blessings of the Everlasting Covenant, which cannot fail.

Once again we stood in awe and wonder as Jesus demonstrated His power. At the moment of receiving, many of the communicants fell down under the power of God and received healing and deliverance. A cripple walked, a blind woman saw, a goitre disappeared, abdominal pains were healed. The blessings of the covenant automatically came upon those who partook of the bread and wine by faith. God's covenant children left the table clothed in robes of righteousness, walking in divine health through the Blood and through the Body of Jesus that was broken so that they could be forgiven and made whole.

On the final night, I spoke about the second coming of Jesus. I told them of the many signs which showed that the time of His return was not far off, and warned about the false christs who the Bible said would appear on earth before that time (Matt. 24:24) and emphasised the Biblical warning that they should not be deceived by these false men, however much they spoke about peace, unity and brotherhood, wonders and miracles (2 Thess. 2:9, Rev. 13:14). It was important that God's people should check all things with the word of God. That night again, at my invitation, many came forward and were born again. As the counsellors were getting their names, so that they could be followed up, I turned to ask those who were sick to come forward for healing. Before I could say anything, one of the ushers waved to me from the crowd. I strained in the glare of the platform lights to see what he was holding. As he got nearer the front, I saw he was leading an elderly lady and waving a surgical brace. They came up to the microphone and he held up the steel and canvas brace. 'Look', he said 'Jesus has already performed a great miracle. This lady was seated in the Grandstand behind you, suddenly the power of God came upon her. She knew Jesus had healed her and she took off the brace.' We gave her the microphone and she spoke in Tagalog. I did not understand what she said but as she pointed to her back and raised her arms and laughed, the message was obvious. I took the microphone and looked out across the crowd of hopeful people and shouted, 'Jesus is no respecter of persons, He loves each of us the same. What he has done for this lady he wants to do for you. All you have to do is to look to Jesus as our sister did; you don't need anyone to lay hands on you. Jesus is the Healer.'

Jesus used the miracle to raise the faith of His people. He loved them. They had repented of their sins, renounced their idolatry and superstitious religion, and now He wanted to shower them with His blessings. He wanted to heal their sick bodies, and those who reached out to Him in faith were healed.

On the previous evening, I had mentioned my concern to Pastor Isaguirre that the new Christians should be baptised. He agreed and we approached the Ministry of Works to see if they could provide a temporary pool at the Grandstand. That, they said would be difficult, but had we thought of using the fountain in the park? We would have no problem because the sprays had been turned off, to save water. So at the close of the last meeting, I quickly changed out of my new red dress and with Pastor Isaguirre, led about seventy people who wanted to be baptised across the park to the fountain. The pastor made it clear that he wanted me to help so I lowered myself into the water. As I disturbed the surface, I became aware that the sprays had been turned off a long time ago and the water had been stagnant and now stank. Pastor Isaguirre seemed unconcerned, so we began to immerse these new brothers and sister. It was late at night by the time the last one had shaken himself dry in the warm air and left for home, rejoicing. As I came, dripping, back to the Grandstand, where the clearing up was still in progress, I was careful to keep to windward of those I spoke to. Next time, and I had a feeling there would be a next time, we would make sure the water was fresh!

Chapter Twenty-two

The face framed in the dark sideburns was grey with fatigue
and pain. It belonged to a Filipino man about twenty-five
years old. He had started on this Good Friday morning
from his village some miles away, to walk to Manila. He
had carried on through the noon heat. In his hand he held a
whip made of ten leather thongs. As he walked, he beat his
bare back and by the time he reached the city it was covered
with red weals, dripping blood. A large crowd had gathered
in the square in front of the church awaiting his arrival. He
had been preceded by others like himself, who arrived at
fifteen minute intervals. When they reached the foot of the
steps, they were received by men and women carrying
whips, before whom they prostrated themselves and were
lashed. They crawled on their knees into the church and
were lashed again. They crawled to the altar, worshipped
the host, then bowed to a group of statues and kissed their
stone feet. All this was accompanied by a choir in the
church, working in shifts, who kept up a continuous chant
throughout the day. But this last man was the one the
crowd had been waiting for. He staggered into the square,
lay on his face and was whipped. Three men dragged
forward a heavy cross stored for the past year and still
stained with the blood of previous victims. The cross was
laid flat on the pavement in front of the church door and the
man allowed himself to be picked up and to be positioned,
arms outstretched on the beams. His arms were secured to
the timber with wide blue bands. His feet were placed on a

small pedestal fixed to the vertical beam and tied in place. A black veil was adjusted over his face and he was given a drink.

I had gone to the square with students from the Bible Training College, with Daphne, and with Phil and Sheila to see for myself how this solemn day was publicly celebrated. Any notion that I was going to see a dramatic performance of the Scriptural events, telling the Bible story in mime, was swiftly dispelled. This was a totally different event, both in presentation and intent, from the mediaeval mystery plays that are still performed in England. I interviewed people in the crowd and Phil recorded their replies. They explained that what we were seeing was the Roman Catholic sacrament of penance, by which these men hoped to receive forgiveness of their sins, through their suffering. They hoped that by it, they and their families would 'have good fortune and be saved from disease'.

I was sickened by the sight and by this distortion of the Gospel, I tried to explain to those I interviewed that we are saved by grace, not by works; that Jesus, the sinless son of God, allowed His blood to be shed as an atonement for our sins, and I showed them the scriptures:

By grace are ye saved through faith: and that not of yourselves: it is the gift of God.

Eph. 2:8

The blood of Jesus Christ His Son cleanseth us from all sin.

1 John 1:7

Only His blood was an acceptable offering, and His blood needed to be offered only once. What these men were doing was an abomination to God; they were denying the sufficiency of the sacrifice of Jesus Christ and the Father's love in offering it freely to sinners. I took a loudhailer and began to preach the truth of the Gospel to the crowd; a few listened and one young man recognised the truth and repented and accepted Jesus as his Saviour.

The man lying spreadeagled and bound to the cross now became the centre of everyone's attention. I could see that he was heavily drugged, his eyes rolling in his head. A hammer and nails were produced and with no sign of the monstrosity of the act, either from the participants or the spectators, a six-inch nail was driven through each of the out-stretched hands, securing them to the cross. The cross with its victim was then hoisted into an upright position and hauled up to the roof of the church where it was fixed and left. He hung there through the long hot afternoon, vainly believing, in his ignorance of the truth, that he was pleasing God. The binding of his arms and the provision of a pedestal would have ensured that he did not hang on the nails and be more seriously injured. We did not wait to see him taken down. We wanted to get away from the scene and pray for him and all the other confused and deceived people in the Philippines, that their eyes would be opened to the truth of the Gospel; the Good News.

I was told that in at least twenty other places in the Philippines similar events took place. To me, this was a positive rejection of the scriptural truth of the Gospel of grace.

Chapter Twenty-three

A bare light bulb clicked into life and illuminated the sleeping children. But it was not they who caught my attention. A young man, his face twisted with pain, was standing in the middle of the room, unable to sleep. He seemed to be wearing an extraordinary garment which, on looking closer, I saw were layers of coconut fibre, bound to his legs by leather thongs. 'This is my friend that I want you to pray for', said the man who had begged me, at the end of the meeting, to come with him. Daphne, who had climbed the rickety ladder behind me, was praying quietly in the Spirit. By now the children were stirring on their straw mats and as I glanced round the room, devoid of furniture, I saw that it was dominated by a portrait hanging on the wall. I knew that they believed this to be a picture of Jesus, but it was horrible. It showed a man with big doleful eyes full of sadness. I turned back to look at the young man, who was now staring at me, wondering why I was there. I spoke to the man who had brought me there, 'Tell him to fetch his parents.' He translated for me, and the young man went into the second room and called them.

As we waited, I asked, 'Why are you wearing coconut fibre on your legs?' 'I have great pain which goes from my feet up into my head and my feet are always icy-cold. The witch doctor came and sacrificed and bound my legs.' 'When did the witch doctor do this?', I enquired. 'Two weeks ago', he replied, 'but it is not much better.' His mother and father appeared and the man who had brought me explained why I was there. By now, all the sleeping children had thrown off their mosquito nets and were sitting up. The whole family listened as I read from Exodus 20:

> Thou shalt not make unto thee any graven image, or any likeness of any thing that is in heaven above, or that is in the water under the earth. Thou shalt not bow down thyself to them, nor serve them; for I the Lord thy God am a jealous God, visiting the iniquity of the fathers upon the children unto the third and fourth generation of them that hate me.
>
> Exod. 20:4, 5

These dear people had no idea that God hated idolatry. They had been bowing down to and praying through their holy pictures and were shocked when they heard the words of Scripture. 'Are you willing to turn from idolatry and tear up these pictures?' I asked. They looked at one another and both nodded their head vigorously and said 'Yes' in unison.

I got on my knees and invited the parents and son to join me, as I led them in a prayer of repentance and renunciation of their idolatry. Jesus forgave them and filled them with the Holy Spirit. We tore the pictures off the walls and the mother took them and the witch doctor's fibre outside, and burned them. I felt joy in my spirit as God's word was obeyed; now I knew that the way was open for the young man's healing, and as God had promised me on the aeroplane, sickness would be taken away, when the idols were broken down and God alone was served and obeyed.

When the mother returned, we cast the evil spirits out of the house in the name of Jesus (for behind every idol is an evil spirit). Daphne and I laid hands on the young man and took authority over the spirits of darkness, that had been attacking his body. In the name of Jesus we set him free from his spiritual connection with the witch doctor and also commanded the chain of generation bondage to idolatry, which held the whole family, to be broken. I laid hands on his feet and as I prayed in the Spirit, his feet grew warm and the pain ceased. There was great rejoicing in the family that night and both Daphne and I were greatly encouraged by this family's willingness to obey the word of God and the operation of the Holy Spirit which flowed from that obedience. We told them about Pastor Calamiong and his students who met nearby. The faithful friend of the family, who had brought me to the home, agreed to call and take them.

Daphne and I, with the help of Pastor Isaguirre had purchased a good second hand jeepney and driven up with Phil and Sheila to the city of Dagupan. We found my old friend Pastor Calamiong and his wife Connie prospering. The Lord had enabled them to move from their former home which was built of bamboo into a new concrete house. Their new house was large enough to provide accommodation for their Bible College. Since my previous visit they had opened fourteen new outstations in the surrounding villages. These were visited weekly by the students who spent Mondays to Fridays being taught and Saturdays and Sundays evangelising at the outstations. These little churches were growing and I was thrilled to hear the stories which the students brought back and to see their zeal for the Lord. They were greatly hampered by lack of transport, having to rely on lifts and walking long distances.

Benji, the sixth son of Pastor Calamiong was my interpreter. He had been born in Baguio, where his father had worked for an insurance company and had come South with the family when his father was called by God to give up his job and start a Bible School. The years in Dagupan since then had not been easy, as his parents committed themselves to the hard work of establishing the school and looking after the students on limited resources. After spending a year as a student in the school, Benji wanted to give up and go back to Baguio with its pleasant climate. His childhood friends were all there and he believed he could get a job and be independent.

This was the position when the Lord had brought me to Dagupan to speak to the students on my first visit to the Philippines and though I did not know it when I arrived, Benji had made up his mind to leave that same day. I had spoken to the students and prayed with many of them, individually, afterwards. Benji had told me what he intended to do and I had a strong impression that here was another, like Jonah, whom God had called and who was trying to run away. He shared with me his problems and the irritations and frustrations he was feeling. In response the Lord put words in my mouth for him. 'Benji', I found myself saying, 'there is a field out there ready to be harvested and you are the one ordained by God to go out there and reap that field. You cannot run away from God for there is no place to hide.' He did not leave as he had planned but came instead to the evening meeting where I preached on the Baptism in the Holy Spirit. When he came forward, Jesus baptised him in the Holy Spirit. As the power of God came upon him, he dropped to his knees, lifted his arms and out of his mouth flowed his new heavenly language. For more than an hour he knelt on the concrete floor, with his arms raised in the air while the Spirit of God interceded for him and dealt with the forces of darkness that were seeking to lead him away from the will of his heavenly Father. He got up a changed man. One month later, the Lord revealed to him that the harvest field was the small island of Pugaro. He went there and for three years preached the Gospel, taught the word of God and reaped the harvest.

Now the Lord had brought him back to Dagupan. He promptly volunteered to interpret for me when, with Pastor Calamiong and a group of students, we visited the out-stations, to minister with them and encourage them to expect a spiritual breakthrough. Everywhere I went, the theme of idolatry kept coming to me. I was, in any case, continually reminded of the extent of this evil. Away from the cities, in the scantily populated mountains the idols were crude, ill-proportioned carved figures of little men with fierce faces. In Dagupan and the surrounding metropolis, every shop had its shrine, with an altar and brightly painted statues of a baby king, of the Virgin Mary and of saints. I guessed most houses, except those of born-again Christians, had them too.

Benji grew in confidence as we progressed round the out-stations. One day the place chosen for the meeting was the small plaza in front of the local church. Through the wrought iron doors we could look into the interior and see people lighting candles and bowing before the idols. Benji looked at me uncertainly. He knew what I had been saying about idolatry in a dozen other meetings at which he had interpreted for me and I guessed that he was wondering if I would take the same line to the people coming out of a church where they had been actually doing it. I think he knew me well enough to be in no doubt that I would not compromise the word of God.

About a hundred people, on their way from church drifted towards where we had set up a lectern and microphones. I began to read from Exodus 20, while a slightly nervous Benji translated. As we began to expound this Scripture about ten people walked away, muttering furiously to show their disagreement. But we continued, with Benji getting bolder every moment, 'God cast the Israelites away from Himself, because they made and bowed down to dumb idols of stone and wood, silver and gold. God gave them many opportunities to repent of their idolatry but they refused to destroy their images, so God scattered them through the nations of the world, where they have been hated and persecuted, through the generations, up to the present day. God used them as an example to the people of the world who choose to walk in disobedience to His word and bow before shameful idols. God is no respecter of persons; if He cast the Israelites away from Himself, because of their idolatry, He will do the same to the people of the Philippine Islands, who continue to bow before images. He will cast you and all the other people of the world who refuse to destroy their shameful idols away from Himself.'

At the end of the meeting, seventy people came forward prepared to renounce idolatry, repent of their sins and make Jesus alone Lord of their life and to prove this by going home and destroying their idols. The students were amazed at the way the people had responded. Where they had expected stony hearts and closed minds, they had seen that the Holy Spirit had already been at work preparing hearts and minds to receive the word of God. This demonstration of what God could do was going to be important for their own ministries and for all those who were going to hear the word of God through them. But for the moment, relief and happiness at the outcome of the day's activities was evident in their smiles and chatter in the ride back to school.

When we arrived they dashed back to their quarters to get ready for the evening meal and I led the way into the front room of the house. In our absence the enemy had struck. I saw Connie's still form lying motionless, face down on the floor. A look of fear and panic passed over Pastor Calamiong's face as he saw his wife's still body. 'It's her heart,' he said, 'she is having a heart attack.' She moaned as we turned her over. I looked down at a face contorted by the violent pain she was suffering. The six people in the room dropped on their knees spontaneously and began to pray in tongues. I rebuked the demon of darkness that was attacking Connie and commanded in the name of Jesus that it desist in this foul attack instantly. She continued to lie on the floor, unable to move or speak. We continued to pray. Ten minutes later, we saw her face change. Pain slipped away and she smiled at us. As we watched she slowly levered herself up into a sitting position then stood up, walked slowly to a couch and lay down.

I knew that for some time she had suffered from a heart condition. The enemy had convinced her that all her hard work over the years, cooking and cleaning for the family and students had weakened her heart. I asked one of the family to get some bread and wine. I sat down on the couch beside Connie and told her, 'There is nothing wrong with your heart except that the enemy has attacked you and he wants you to believe that you have a bad heart condition. The devil is a liar and a thief. You must not believe him. You must believe the word of God. God has made an Everlasting Covenant with you through the blood and body of Jesus. All your needs were met through Him at Calvary. The Covenant cannot fail if entered into by faith.' She received the bread and believed that it represented the body of Jesus that was broken for her so that she at all times could live in divine health. She totally trusted and was completely healed. Next day, she was back, fully involved in all the work of house and school, and we were able to take to the road again with the students. As we drove around the villages all the manifestations of idolatry made me realise how superstition and 'religiosity' were ruling the lives of people, and why, therefore, there was such poverty and disease. The blessings of God could only flow, bringing health and prosperity, to those who walked in obedience to His word. The evidence of this was visible on a national scale, but it was when I met the consequences in the life of an individual, that I was struck by the full horror of the results of bowing down to images. An example was the boy who had to be tied down.

We went to his home at his mother's request, to pray for him. It turned out to be a flourishing shop selling musical instruments. She brought us into a ground floor room where we saw a distressing sight. A handsome, healthy sixteen-year-old boy lay on a bed frame. His feet were secured to the bottom rail and a broad leather strap passed over his chest and under the frame so that he could not rise. He was struggling violently against the restraints and alternately moaning and shrieking. My heart filled with compassion for him. 'He is mad', his mother said softly, 'and the doctors cannot help. Whenever a missionary comes, I ask him to visit and to pray. There is always an improvement afterwards, but it does not last. Will you pray for him, please?' The most prominent object in that well-furnished room was an expensively framed idol of the Virgin Mary and the crowned baby Jesus which they call St Ninian. I opened my Bible to read Exodus 20. As I went through verses 4 and 5 her face hardened and I knew she was resisting the Word of God. But I continued, and explained to her that her own son was mentally deranged because of generations of idolatry. I assured her that the blessing of God would come on her house and her family if she would smash her idols and repent of her sins. I had no doubt in my spirit that this was so. 'If you smash these idols, God will prove to you that His Word is true, by healing your son,' I said with emphasis.

Her reaction was immediate, but she tried to hide the anger that I could see in her eyes. She shook her head. I tried again. 'The Lord says that He will visit the iniquity of the fathers upon the children through to the fourth generation of those who hate Him, but show mercy to the thousands of those who love Him and keep His commandments. If we love Jesus we will keep His commandments. He has warned us, commanded us, that we are to have no other gods before Him. We must not make idols of His mother or the saints. We must not bow down before idols of any kind. God hates idolatry.' I could see she was too angry to hear, but she kept herself under control. Her statues were more important to her than the Word of God and were really gods in her life. I continued, 'You told me that many missionaries had come and prayed for your son; after each visit and prayer he improved for a short time and then grew much worse. Your son is possessed by evil spirits, and those spirits are controlling his life because he has been brought up within a family of idol worshippers; generations of idol worshippers have caused your son to become insane.'

She looked down at her arms, 'Do you see my arms?' she said. They were badly marked. 'What caused the marks?' I asked. 'They are bites; my son has often attacked me and bitten me when I release him. He is getting too strong for me and I have to keep him tied up until his father comes home.' And then, pleadingly, she said, 'Please pray for him that he may get even a little better.' 'If you smash those idols, and repent of idolatry, I will pray for him and Jesus will heal him,' I said again. 'I cannot smash my beautiful Mother and Saints' she replied. 'Let me tell you why your son became a little better and then worse after missionaries prayed for him. They cast out the evil spirits that were ruling him, but because of idolatry in this home, seven more spirits have taken possession of him causing him to become worse. If you smash the idols, I will cast the demons out of your house and out of your son in the name of Jesus, and Jesus will fill him with the Holy Spirit.'

During this conversation, the shrieks and screams were becoming louder and the boy's struggling more violent, as the demons reacted to what was being said. She did not reply. I got up from my chair and moved towards the altar. 'If you yourself, can't smash these idols, let me do it,' I suggested. She grabbed me by the arm, 'No, no, please don't,' she said. My heart sank. God has given everyone free will, and anyone who chooses, in their own wilfulness to walk in disobedience to His Word, must bear the consequences. I did not want to give up. I walked over to the boy and attempted to lay my hand on his forehead. He shook his head violently, and made noises like a wild animal. I yielded my voice to the Holy Spirit and prayed in tongues. 'You should know,' I said following the prompting of the Spirit, 'that Jesus loves you and your son. He wants to set him free, please submit your life to Jesus and be filled with the Spirit.' 'Yes, please tell me how', she said. I began to lead her in a prayer of repentance, but when we came to asking the Lord to forgive her for the sin of idolatry, she could go no further. She wanted salvation, she wanted Jesus, she wanted to be filled with the Spirit, but more than any of these she wanted her idol gods.

'Look' I said, 'for years you have been bowing down before those idols and praying for your son. Your prayers have not been answered, because there is only one mediator between man and God and He is Jesus Christ. God has forbidden us to be involved in any way with the spirits of dead people. For your son's sake, just smash those idols and try God's way.' She shook her head and looked away. We got up and left the house with heavy hearts. The animal-like sounds from the bedroom followed us out, as if the demons were shouting their defiance. I looked back and saw the mother standing by the door. I would try one more time. I walked back and said to her 'When you are ready to smash those idols send a message to me and I will come from wherever I am and pray for your son and Jesus will heal him'. She smiled at me, and I smiled back. I laid my hand on her shoulder and in Jesus' name, bound the demons that held her captive, then turned and walked away.

Every day we expected to hear from the woman, but no message came. The Lord had called Sheila to a ministry of intercession, which she faithfully followed, and one afternoon when I was praying with her, she said, 'The Lord has given me a word in Ezekiel 14:3–8 and I believe it is for the mother of the boy who was tied up'. I opened my Living Bible and read:

> These men worship idols in their hearts – should I let them ask me anything? Tell them, the Lord God says: I the Lord will personally deal with anyone in Israel who worships idols and then comes to ask my help. For I will punish the minds and hearts of those who turn from me to idols. Therefore warn them that the Lord God says: Repent and destroy your idols, and stop worshipping them in your hearts. I the Lord will personally punish everyone, whether people of Israel or the foreigners living among you, who rejects me for idols and then comes to a prophet to ask for help and advice. I will turn upon him and make a terrible example of him, destroying him; and you shall know I am the Lord.
>
> Ezek. 14:3–8

This Scripture was even more urgent against idolatry than anything I had said to her, and I believed it was the Lord's will that I drew it to her attention. So I wrote it out and included it in a letter, assuring her that Jesus was full of mercy and compassion, and would forgive her if she was willing to walk in obedience to His Word. We sent the letter by hand, hoping that the messenger would return with a request for us to visit. But sadly, the answer was still no. The memory of that young man's torment stayed with me all the time I was in the Philippines and increased the abhorrence I felt for the statues and pictures that confronted me everywhere. In shops, taxis, schools, offices and houses there were these manifestations which I knew now tended to produce, not faith in God, but the exact opposite. Through ignorance of the commandments of God, millions had fallen into the most serious error.

Chapter Twenty-four

'You must utterly destroy their idols.' That was the commission which the Lord had given me on the way to the Philippines. He continued to remind me of it by bringing my attention to what His Word had to say about it. As I became sensitive to the way He looked at idolatry, my heart was continually moved by the plight of the people of that beautiful country. Many were unaware that the veneration they gave to statues and pictures by making them, admiring them, presenting them with offerings of money and flowers, kissing them, bowing to them and praying to or through them, was separating them from God's care and protection. Everywhere I went, God was opening my eyes to these practices and to their consequences.

It was the theme that was laid on my heart, when I spoke to the students at Manila Bible Training Centre. 'Out there,' I told them, 'people you and I love are being lost. They need to see the reality of God in your ministry. You go and cast out demons in the name of Jesus, lay hands on the sick and see them recover. But do not be in two minds about idolatry. God has given us the example of Israel to show what happens when a nation descends into persistent idolatry. They suffered defeat, famine, tribulation and exile. So it is important that you have no doubt about it, so that you can proclaim boldly God's abhorrence of the worship of anything other than Himself'. I prayed with many of them after the meeting for boldness and they fell under the power of God as His Spirit ministered to them.

Some of the students came with me to bring the Gospel to a leper colony which was like a fenced-off town. Twenty-six thousand families lived there, and it is not unusual to find up to ten children in one family. They were separated from the rest of the country, to prevent the disease spreading. We concentrated on the hospital, where the worst affected sufferers were treated. As I walked into the entrance hall, I was horrified to see that it had the same large idols that had been the object of worship in the church where the 'crucifixion' had taken place.

The stench of death and rotting flesh was almost unbearable. I was filled with dismay as I looked upon the remains of human bodies that had been ravaged by leprosy. Some had no fingers, others had no feet – just stumps where the limbs had rotted away. The rest of their flesh was often just a mass of black sores. Others had flat faces because the bones in their noses had rotted away leaving only holes.

It was horrific. Only Satan himself could be responsible for disfiguring God's beautiful creation, man, in this way. I fought back the tears, trying not to show how horrified I was. My heart was bursting with compassion for these people who were rocking to and fro in such pain and agony. It was almost more than I could bear. The whole atmosphere of the place was profoundly sad. We went around the beds and spoke individually to those who would listen, and Daphne and the students sang and ministered with me.

Phil and Sheila came along and recorded the visit. Their microphone captured the sound of a wonderful manifestation of God's power; the thrilling words, 'Jesus is my Lord'. The words were said by a man whose vocal cords had been eaten away by the disease and he had not been able to speak for some time. He lay back in bed, barely moving, clutching the bed cover and holding it so that we should not see his disfigured body. At first I wondered whether he understood, as my companions translated for me. Like so many of the patients he had a number of wall plaques which he venerated. I read the first and second commandment from Exodus 20. I explained the Gospel, that Jesus had shed His blood for him, to pay the price for his sin. That if he believed, and made Jesus his Lord, he would be forgiven and God's Spirit would dwell in him. I explained that he could not make Jesus Lord of his life and at the same time worship or pray through idols. If he smashed his idols and confessed Jesus as Lord, I assured him that Jesus would heal him. I asked him to nod if he was prepared to allow us to destroy his plaques. There was a pause and I wondered whether he had heard. I longed for him to say yes, knowing that Jesus loved him and was pouring that love through us. It was a moment of triumph when he nodded. We broke the idols. I turned to the interpreter and said 'Now tell him to say, Jesus is my Lord'. As the old man opened his mouth, instead of the former incoherent rasping sound he clearly spoke. God had given him new vocal cords. I prayed and cut him free from the spiritual bondage of generations of idol worship and told the leprosy to depart from his body, in the name of Jesus. I asked him to stretch his hand out so that I could shake it to greet him as a brother in Christ.

Some wanted to have a theological argument with me, some were so sure that God had sent their disease that they could not agree that we could ask Him to take it away, others were reluctant to smash their idols. However, I remember a few who received what I said and were obedient and repented and asked Jesus to come into their life as their Lord. These, I am sure, received the Lord's healing. In one case it was manifested on the spot. A tall thin man, whom I felt from the beginning, really wanted to know God, listened carefully to what I had to say. When I asked him about idols, he was the only one I talked to who had none. And he had a Bible! The interpreter led him in a prayer of repentance and he was born again. He had been infected for three years and he had pain in his trunk, in his arm and hands. He was unable to raise his arms or clench his fist, but when we prayed the pain went and he recovered full movement.

We then went into a large ward of about thirty beds. The floor was dirty. The wooden stands that served as bedside tables were filthy as were the bedcovers. Cobwebs hung around the dim lights, lizards darted around, catching the flies that were trapped in the cobwebs. I presented the Gospel and stressed the sin of idolatry. When I asked those who were prepared to repent and make Jesus alone their Lord to raise their hands, they painfully responded by raising blackened stumps of arms or legs or whatever they could, and I realised that I had made the request without fully realising the pain and determination required to make that response.

When I asked if they wished me to ask the staff to remove the idols from the hallway, all except two agreed. The nurse in charge was staggered at this request and hastened to explain that only the Matron could authorise such a serious action, and she was away. In obedience to the great commission I went round the beds and laid hands on each individual except the two dissenters, and prayed that Jesus would take away their pain.

I was beginning to get to know the students at the Bible Training Centre as individuals and to share with them some of the messages which God had given me for the Philippines. I saw that they really wanted to go out and tell their fellow countrymen about a Jesus who was alive today and loved them and was calling them to repent and be born again. They were being well taught by Pastor Isaguirre and his staff. I took every opportunity to invite them to go with me, so they would be encouraged to expect that, as they themselves preached the full Gospel, the Lord would confirm His Word with signs and miracles. And those miracles would include God's provision for their material needs.

A complete reliance on missionaries from the West, whether short or long stay, could never be the answer to full scale evangelism of the country. An obvious reason was that there would never be enough of them. Less obviously, but even more important, was that the presence of missionaries from abroad with resources and a high degree of personal commitment and even an apparently more powerful ministry, could persuade the local church that they were too constrained by poverty and lack of spiritual power to attempt much themselves. I had discovered from personal experience what a hindrance lack of transport could be, so having learned that lesson, I was not surprised that God chose to meet that need through me. I knew He wanted to provide a fleet of jeepneys to increase the effectiveness of the pastors and their students and to enable them to go into even more remote areas. I had no money of my own and I was averse to making appeals, but I knew that because He wanted those vehicles in the Philippines, He would provide the means, and time will reveal His perfect purposes.

I was privileged that the Lord had sent me to work with people who really wanted to move forward. He did not lead me to stay on a long-term basis, but I knew that part of my calling was to encourage and build up His people so that they would be more fully equipped. I had a deep desire in my heart that they should understand that there was nothing special about me, that God was no respecter of persons, that the Holy Spirit in them was the same Holy Spirit as in me and that they too

might know what is the exceeding greatness of his power to usward who believe, according to the working of his mighty power . . .'

Eph. 1:19

ISABEL CHAPMAN MINISTRIES

Video Tape Catalogue

V.T.1. O, Ye Dry Bones!
– Explanation of how fear and unbelief limits God demonstrating His power.

V.1. Testimony
– Testimony and explanation of the fall of man. Satan's defeat and man's restoration.

V.2. His Mercies Endureth For Ever
– Cleansing and healing for all.

V.T.3. Our Comforter – The Holy Spirit
– The baptism of the Holy Spirit, the reasons for, and importance of, praying in tongues.

V.3. By His Stripes We Are Healed
– Comprehensive teaching on the healing that Jesus accomplished for us at Calvary.

V.4. Our Covenant With God
– The full significance of the Lord's Supper explained.

V.5. Does God Heal Everyone?
– Some reasons why some are healed and others not.

V.6. Obedience to the Word
– Accepting the word of God and acting upon it.

V.8. Thou Shalt Have No Other Gods
– Laying down the things of this world in which our confidences lie.

V.7. The Power of Words
– Why what we say is so important.

V.T.6. A Chosen People
– Preparation of the overcomers.

V.9. The Last Days
– A general explanation of the times in which we live.

V.10. Have You Ears to Hear?
– What the Spirit is saying to the Churches.

V.11. The Seven Trumpets
– The End Times with special reference to the Children of Israel.

V.12. The Seven Seals
– Reveals the different stages in the career of the Anti-Christ.

V.13. Freed from Occult Bondages

V.15. Come Out of Her, My People!
– Comparing the doctrine of Rome with the Word of God.

Philippine Films

P.1. Children of the Philippines I
– Introductory film of the life-style of the Filipino Children.

P.2. Children of the Philippines II
– The baptism of the Holy Spirit amongst born-again children.

P.3. Teenagers of the Philippines
– The outpouring and the work of the Holy Spirit amongst teenagers.

> All
> on
> one
> tape
> (£15 + £1)

P.4. Ministry in Lewan
– Journey to Lewan and the work of the Holy Spirit in a jungle area.

P.5. Sumadel
– Life and ministry in a primitive village high in the mountains.

P.6. Visit to a Leper Colony
– Miracles amongst the lepers and the abominations that bring disease and poverty upon a nation. (Parents! – please view before showing children.)

P.7. Signs and Wonders at Quirino Grandstand
– Miraculous display of God's Covenant Power.

1. Tapes may be hired for £5 per tape per week plus £1 p&p total £6.
2. If you wish to purchase a tape having seen it, please send a further £10 within the due date.
3. Purchase price of each tape £15 plus £1 p&p, total £16.

ISABEL CHAPMAN MINISTRIES A/V DEPT.
Underfield Greenodd Nr. Ulverston Cumbria LA12 8HU

VIDEO-TAPE ORDER AND HIRE FORM

Please state:

TAPE No.	TITLE	BUY	HIRE	V.H.S. Beta or 2,000

NAME AND ADDRESS ....
(BLOCK CAPITALS PLEASE)

.... Tel. No..........

I enclose cheque/PO for .... Signed ....

Our prayer is that you will be blessed and that God will be glorified in and through these tapes.

Audio Tape Catalogue

A1 Testimony I
Includes Isabel's conversion and her initial visit to the Philippine Islands.

A2 Testimony II
Includes Isabel's latest visit to the Philippine Islands.

A3 By His Stripes We Are Healed
Comprehensive teaching on what Jesus accomplished for us at Calvary.

A4 Our Covenant With God
The full significance of the Lord's Supper explained.

A5 God's Plan of Redemption
The fall of man, Satan's defeat and man's restoration.

A6 Obedience to the Word
Accepting the Word of God as true and acting upon it.

A8 Thou Shalt Have No Other Gods
Do you have other gods in your life?

A9 The Last Days
A general explanation of the times in which we are living.

A10 The Mark of the Beast
The End Times with special reference to the impending cashless society.

A11 The Seven Trumpets
The End Times with special reference to the exodus of the Jews from Russia.

A12 Days of Preparation
Warning that we are in the last of the Last Days and explanation of how and why to prepare ourselves.

A13 Our Heavenly Language
The baptism of the Holy Spirit, the reasons for, and the importance of, praying in tongues.

A14 Our Family Physician
Dr. Jesus: the greatest physician in all the world.

A15 Come Out of Her, My People!
Comparing the doctrine of Rome with the Word of God.

Recent Additions:

A16 Does God Heal Everyone?

A17 The Seven Seals
Reveals the different stages in the career of the Anti-Christ.

A18 Be Not Deceived
Beware the New Age Movement.

A19 Having Done All – Stand!
Being affected by only that which is written in the Word.

A20 Beware Ecumenism

A21 God Hates Idolatry

Music Tape

M3 Praise and Worship

Books

Arise and Reap
£1.95 (+40p p&p)

Reaping with Joy
£2.50 (+40p p&p)

All proceeds from the sale of these tapes go towards
providing Jeeps for Pastors in the Philippines to take
the Gospel of Jesus Christ to outlying districts.

Thank you for your support.
Yours in Jesus' Service,
Isabel Chapman

ISABEL CHAPMAN MINISTRIES A/V DEPT.
Underfield Greenodd Nr. Ulverston Cumbria LA12 8HU

AUDIO ORDER FORM

Please complete this form and send it to the above address together with the costs.

AUDIOTAPE ....
(Name and number of tape)

NAME AND ADDRESS......................................
(Block letters please)

....

Prices: Audiotapes –   £3.00 (+35p p&p)
        Reaping with Joy £2.50 (+40p p&p)
        Arise and Reap   £1.95 (+40p p&p)
        Complete set of   I enclose a cheque for.....
        Audiotapes –   £55 (+£3.00 p&p)
        (20 Teaching and 1 Music)   Signed ....

Our prayer is that you will be blessed and that God will be glorified in and through these tapes.